MAPLE LEAF FOREVER?

THE WARTS & ALL STORY OF CANADA'S CREATION

Written by Paul Keery
Illustrated by Mike Wyatt

JackFruit Press Ltd.

Credits:
JackFruit Press Ltd. would like to thank Library and Archives Canada for the photograph on page 29 (G.P. Roberts/LAC/C-000733); Confederation Life/Rogers Inc for permission to reproduce the painting on page 33 and Canadian Press (Ron Poling) for the image on page 54. We would also like to express our gratitude to Paul Heersink of Rand McNally Canada for preparing the maps on pages 8, 44, 58 and 60.

Text © 2008 Paul Keery
Illustrations © 2008 Michael Wyatt

JackFruit Press Ltd.
Orangeville, Ontario, Canada
www.jackfruitpress.com

Library and Archives Canada Cataloguing in Publication

Keery, Paul, 1958–
    Maple leaf forever?: the warts & all story of Canada's creation / written by Paul Keery; illustrated by Mike Wyatt.

Includes bibliographical references and index.
ISBN 978-1-897325-19-3

1. Canada–History–Confederation, 1867–Juvenile literature.
2. Constitutional history–Canada–Juvenile literature. I. Wyatt, Mike, 1953– II. Title.

FC470.K43 2008   j971.04'9   C2008-900048-X

Printed and bound in Canada

Canada Council   **Conseil des Arts**
for the Arts   **du Canada**

We acknowledge the support of the Canada Council for the Arts which last year invested $20.1 million in writing and publishing throughout Canada.

Mixed Sources
Product group from well-managed forests and recycled wood or fibre
www.fsc.org Cert no. SGS-COC-004659
© 1996 Forest Stewardship Council

FSC

To my parents, Nan and Steve Keery,

whose love for books and history is reflected in these pages.

– Paul Keery

To my wife Janet and my children Tyler and Madeline.

– Mike Wyatt

HOW TO USE THIS BOOK

KEEP AN EYE OUT FOR THESE SPECIAL FEATURES:

JUST WHAT MIGHT OUR PAST LEADERS THINK OF CANADA AS IT IS TODAY? LOOK AT THESE FEATURES, INTERSPERSED THROUGHOUT THE BOOK, AND WE'LL TELL YOU!

STATE OF THE UNION?

WHAT IF?

THESE ORIGINAL CARTOON STRIPS CHALLENGE YOU TO IMAGINE DIFFERENT OUTCOMES TO HISTORICAL EVENTS

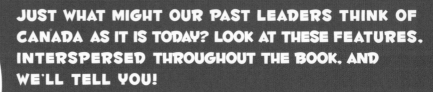

... THE BATTLE OF GETTYSBURG ... CH IT WON IN ACTUAL HISTORY, ALLOWING THE NORTH TO KEEP FIGHTING). PRESIDENT LINCOLN MUST ADMIT THE CIVIL WAR IS OVER; THE **USA** HAS LOST.

TODAY, JANUARY 1ST, 1863, WE RECOGNIZE THE **CONFEDERATE STATES OF AMERICA** AS A NEW NATION, SEPARATE FROM THE UNITED STATES.

AFRAID THAT BRITAIN WILL HELP THE **CSA** BY ATTACKING FROM CANADA, THE **USA** PUTS A STRONG ARMY AND NAVY ON THE BORDER. TRADE IS REDUCED TO LIMIT VISITORS FROM CANADA, WHO COULD BE **CSA** SPIES.

IN 1866, THE UNITED STATES CONGRESS OFFERS THE BRITISH NORTH AMERICA COLONIES MONEY, INVESTMENTS IN BETTER RAILWAYS, AND AGREES TO PAY ANY DEBTS THE COLONIES OWE IF THEY JOIN THE UNITED STATES.

1866
AN INVITATION
TO CANADA TO
JOIN THE
UNITED STATES

SURELY YOU CAN DEFEND US FROM THE USA!

NOT AGAINST A TWO MILLION MAN ARMY. YOU ARE ON YOUR OWN.

UNABLE TO REFUSE, CANADA JOINS THE USA ON JULY 1ST, 1867. PRESIDENT LINCOLN ABOLISHES SLAVERY AND DECLARES A "FREE NATION", UNLIKE THE **CSA**, WHICH ALLOWS SLAVERY.

TABLE OF CONTENTS

P.31

P.26

P.38

P.67

INTRODUCTION: A NEW NATION?

Monday, July 1, 1867. From Sarnia in the west to Halifax in the east, it was the very first Canada Day—though it wouldn't be called that for more than 100 years. George Brown spoke for four million newly minted Canadians in his newspaper, the *Toronto Globe*, when he wrote, "we hail this birthday of a new nationality." They had picnics, parades, speeches, and fireworks. They were going to build a nation that would take its place in the world.

Could such a big country actually work? The leaders of the old Province of Canada (the area we know today as Quebec and Ontario, but joined together) spent all their time fighting with each other instead of making decisions for the good of the people. Could more leaders, in a bigger country, get along well enough to make good laws to help the people?

Could people from the old colonies of Nova Scotia, New Brunswick, and the Province of Canada really become proud Canadians, or would they always be more loyal to their home provinces?

In 1866, the United States had offered to let the British North American colonies join the union. Could this new country stand on its own, or would it someday join the United States?

Think of Canada today. Aren't we still looking to answer these same questions?

The leaders who met to build the new country had their own answers for their own time.

John A. Macdonald and George Brown of Canada West did.

So did George-Étienne Cartier of Canada East.

As did Charles Tupper and Joseph Howe of Nova Scotia.

Not to mention Leonard Tilley of New Brunswick.

Only one problem: they didn't agree on the answers! They argued and fought for three years, in meeting rooms and dance halls, over plenty of food and drink, to find these answers. Macdonald flattered and cajoled to push his dream to reality. Macdonald had help. Some say that money talked, that Macdonald and Tilley bribed New Brunswick voters to support Confederation. Others say that it was the fear of invasion from the United States— because of the Fenian raids in 1866—that made the colonies agree to join. It's even said that Britain pushed the reluctant Atlantic colonies into joining Confederation because the British, too, were scared of the United States.

> EVERYONE HAD QUESTIONS ABOUT HOW THE NEW COUNTRY COULD WORK. ONLY ONE PROBLEM: THEY DIDN'T AGREE ON THE ANSWERS!

In early 1867, Canada's constitution was written. A constitution is a set of rules that explains how a country works. These rules are called laws—the most important laws of any country. Canada would have one national government and four local governments for each of the four colonies, which would now be called "provinces."

Queen Victoria was happy about this—and she liked Macdonald very much. She knighted him because he was the most important of all the leaders who had created Canada. This meant that he would now be called Sir John A. Macdonald. The other leaders were unhappy that they hadn't been given the same honour— they thought they had done just as much as Macdonald to create the new country.

Macdonald became Canada's first prime minister. People couldn't imagine that anyone else could be its leader. Even Brown, Tupper, and Cartier had to accept that.

Macdonald was pleased. He knew that there is a difference between what a law says and how it will actually be obeyed, because some words in the law will mean different things to different people. This is why we have lawyers and judges; they interpret the exact meaning of the laws we have to obey.

Macdonald knew that the new provincial leaders—the premiers of the provinces—would try to use the rules in the constitution to make the provinces stronger than the new national government. As prime minister, he could protect his dream of Canada, and make sure that the new government— and the new Canada—would be much stronger than the provinces.

But Macdonald had forgotten about Oliver Mowat, the second premier of Ontario, who had a different dream of Canada. Mowat fought Macdonald for nearly 20 years—and finally won. Macdonald was angry. But more was at stake than his ego.

It was a fight that made Canada the country you live in today.

> I KNEW THOSE PREMIERS WOULD GET TOO BIG FOR THEIR BRITCHES! NOW THEY THINK THEY'RE JUST AS GOOD AS THE PRIME MINISTER!
>
> - SIR JOHN A. MACDONALD

STATE OF THE UNION?

POLITICAL DEADLOCK IN THE CANADAS

BRITISH NORTH AMERICA 1866

GREENLAND (Denmark)

ALASKA (Russia)

THE NORTH WESTERN TERRITORIES

NEWFOUNDLAND

BRITISH COLUMBIA

Fort Edmonton

RUPERT'S LAND

St. John's

Victoria • Vancouver

PRINCE EDWARD ISLAND

NEW BRUNSWICK   NOVA SCOTIA

Québec City

Fort Garry •

PROVINCE OF CANADA

Halifax

Montréal

UNITED STATES OF AMERICA

Toronto

They were hopelessly mismatched, but they'd been put together in the hope that one would absorb the other.

UPPER CANADA

Upper Canada (known today as southern Ontario) was thoroughly English and Protestant. Optimistic, prosperous, with a rapidly growing population, its people had their eyes set on expansion into new territories north and west of the Great Lakes. The future looked bright.

LOWER CANADA

Lower Canada (today's southern Quebec) had been captured from France by Britain in 1763. Since then, the English-Canadian minority had dominated the French-Canadian majority. A French-Canadian rebellion against English-Canadian rule had failed in 1837. The French Canadians wanted only to survive with their culture, language, and Catholic religion intact. The future looked gloomy.

The two colonies merged in 1841 as part of a plan to turn the French-Canadian majority in Lower Canada into a minority in the combined Province of Canada. It was expected that,

REP BY POP

Unhappiness turned to frustration in the 1850s as Canada West grew. In 1853, Reform party leader George Brown first suggested that representation by population, or Rep by Pop, be used to decide how many members each of the two Canadas would have in the legislative assembly. As Canada West possessed a larger population, it would have more seats. A party that won most of its seats in Canada West would be able to form the government without a lot of members from Canada East—and those members would probably be English, not French.

This idea upset the French. A government made mostly of English members from the two Canadas would not care much about the future of French heritage.

when this happened, French Canadians would give up their heritage and be assimilated into English culture.

POPULATION SHIFTS IN THE CANADAS

In the 1840s, Canada East (as Lower Canada was now known) had a slightly larger population than Canada West (the new name for Upper Canada). In the 1850s, this changed. Canada West's population became much larger than Canada East's—and would continue to grow. But French Canadians refused to become part of the broader whole and did what they could to protect themselves. Meanwhile, English Canadians grew more and more frustrated with French Canadians, whom they felt were holding back Canada West by spending tax money collected from the larger population there.

By the mid-1860s, union between the two Canadas had broken down. Frustration with the way governments were elected, especially in Canada West, made it too hard to form a government that could make decisions.

DEADLOCK

What caused the political deadlock?

1. After responsible government was introduced into the Legislative Assembly in 1848, the government had to have the almost-impossible support of over half of the members of the Assembly.

2. No single political party was ever elected to a majority government.

3. The partnerships that Canada East and Canada West party leaders made to have enough seats to form a government fell apart when the leaders disagreed with each other, often over the representation by population issue.

HOW GOVERNMENT WORKED

When the two Canadas were joined in 1841, each was given 42 members, or seats, in the new 84-member legislative assembly. But French Canadians suggested that Canada East be given more seats, as it had a larger population at the time.

Neither Great Britain nor Canada West wanted to do this. They wanted the number of seats to be the same. If the 42 English members from Canada West teamed up with the English members from Canada East—usually about one-quarter to one-half of its 42—the English would dominate.

POLITICAL PARTIES EMERGE

But this didn't happen. Instead, two main parties emerged in Canada West: the Conservative party, which would eventually be led by John A. Macdonald, and the Reform party (better known as the Clear Grits), led by George Brown. These two parties disagreed about almost everything: spending, religion, education—and whether the union should be changed because Canada West was growing larger than Canada East. Parties also appeared in Canada East: *les rouges*, liberal reformers who would be led by Antoine-Aimé Dorion in the 1850s and 1860s; and *les bleus*, Canada East's conservatives, led by George-Étienne Cartier in the same period. Unlike the Conservatives and the Reformers, les rouges and les bleus were able to work together to protect French language, culture, and religion.

This situation gave Canada East control of the government: its elected members would always support the party from Canada West that would do the most to help the French. It worked—barely— while the two had roughly the same population.

Still, many people living in Canada West were not very happy about it. Why should the French in Canada East—a minority— control the government?

THE SYSTEM BREAKS DOWN

By the mid-1850s, Macdonald and Cartier had formed a team.

Even so, by the summer of 1858, the political system was breaking down. On July 29, the Macdonald-Cartier ministry was forced to resign from office as it lost the support of the majority of members of the legislative assembly. Brown, together with Dorion, formed a new ministry on August 2.

However, under the rules in 1858, all new government ministers had to resign their seats in the legislative assembly and run for re-election. Because a minister would be working in government and have less time to look after the people in his riding, voters had to agree to it.

So Brown, Dorion, and the ministry members resigned to run in by-elections.

Macdonald and Cartier, who were afraid of what might happen to French-English relations if Brown and Dorion were to govern—and who wanted their old offices back—saw that their parties now had more members in the legislative assembly than their opponents, whose ministers had resigned.

Macdonald and Cartier forced the Brown-Dorion government to resign on August 4 and formed a new ministry two days later. Each minister took an office that was different from the one he'd had on July 29. Under the rules, they would have to resign as well to run in by-elections.

MACDONALD PULLS A FAST ONE!

But Macdonald was sneaky—he knew the rules better than anyone did. Another rule said that in a shuffle—when a minister resigned from one office and took another within a month—the minister did not have to resign and run in a by-election.

So Macdonald, Cartier, and the rest of their ministers all shuffled: they resigned from their new offices on August 7 and took their old offices back. Macdonald had been premier on July 29; on August 6, he returned as deputy premier and then resigned and became premier again on August 7.

DOUBLE SHUFFLE

This was called the "double shuffle." It was legal, but sneaky and underhanded. Brown and his supporters in Canada West were furious, but Brown and Dorion never came close to forming a ministry again.

Canada West's voters stayed angry: they gave more seats to the Reformers in each election. In 1862, the Conservatives won so few seats that, even with the bleu seats in Canada East, the Macdonald-Cartier team did not have a majority and could no longer form the government.

But Brown couldn't form a government either. His Reformers needed the rouges to vote with them and the rouges wouldn't do it. Brown had made it clear that he resented Canada East's control over Canada West. Why, Brown asked, shouldn't Canada East use its own money to pay for whatever it wanted instead of using tax money collected from Canada West's citizens? Why should politicians from Canada East make decisions about education and religious schools in Canada West?

He wanted this to stop. The rouges wanted to keep these policies, however; it was only the bleus and Conservatives they wanted to get rid of. So the Reformers and the rouges could not try again to form a ministry as they did in 1858.

DOUBLE MAJORITY

A weak ministry led by John Sandfield Macdonald was formed in 1862. It tried to govern by setting up the rule of the *double majority*. Under this rule, a simple majority of the whole assembly—42 votes out of 82—would not be enough. Twenty-two members from each of Canada East and West would have to vote for a law for it to pass. This was meant to ensure that both Canada East and Canada West supported the policy. But it was hard to get a majority in both Canadas to agree all the time. The people of Canada West were tired of living in a system they found unworkable, and the double majority was the last straw for them. This government stepped down in June 1864. What would happen now?

BROWN SWEPT AWAY!

TEAMING UP!

The Province of Canada had become impossible to govern. No party or parties could win enough seats to control the legislative assembly.

Canada West's voters no longer believed in the Province of Canada. They felt it was holding them back by giving too much power to the French in Canada East.

It was time for new ideas.

One idea was to break the province into two parts. Canada East and Canada West would be split into a federation of two provinces, each with its own government for education, language, and culture. A federal government would deal with trade and defence.

Many did not like this idea. It seemed to be a lot of trouble to change little. Wouldn't the federal legislative assembly have the same problems as the existing one, if there had to be the same number of members from each province? George Brown had another idea.

BROWN'S GREATEST SPEECH

On June 22, 1864, George Brown spoke in the legislative assembly to convince French Canadians to join the Great Coalition.

"We have two races, two languages, two systems of religious belief, two sets of laws, two systems of everything ... party alliances are one thing, and the interests of my country another ... let us try to rise superior to the pitifulness of party politics ... let us unite to consider and settle this question as a great national issue, in a manner worthy of us as a people."

Brown saw that the French Canadians were taking a great risk. Many French Canadians feared that, in a new country with even more English in it, the risk of assimilation was high. Brown thought that they were brave to agree to the new plan, and said so:

"But it is a great thing, a most bold and manly thing ... for the member for Montreal East (George-Étienne Cartier) to take up the question."

Some of the French-Canadian members were so moved by Brown's speech that they came up to him and kissed him on both cheeks.

COMMITTEE RECOMMENDS CONFEDERATION

In March 1864, he convinced the legislative assembly to create a committee to study the question of federation as a way to end the political deadlock. In June 1864, the committee,

with members from all parties, agreed that federation was a way to solve the problem. Its idea, which had come up before, was not just to split up the two Canadas, but to join all the British colonies in North America into one nation—Confederation. This led to the creation of the Great Coalition.

In 1862 and 1863, John A. Macdonald had asked Brown if he'd be willing to join a coalition with Macdonald and Cartier, so that all the parties would join to form a ministry and each would have some role in the government. Brown had been interested but the talks had failed.

Now, with the political system deadlocked, even Governor General Charles Stanley Monck urged Brown to join with Macdonald and Cartier to form a ministry that could recreate Canada.

Brown agreed. He was still not friendly with Macdonald, but saw that the time had come to put his country first.

While the Reformers were happy, Macdonald had some problems with his fellow Conservatives in Canada West. Despite the kisses, they were not happy to be working with George Brown, who ridiculed them in his newspaper, the *Globe*. They also feared that they would lose elections in a new Ontario, no longer joined to Canada East, to the Reformers.

But most followed Macdonald, realizing that the deadlock could not be allowed to go on.

In Canada East, *bleu* supporters trusted Cartier. They were sure Cartier would not agree to any changes that would hurt French Canadians. The *rouges*, however, were shocked; they thought that Brown had kissed them off. English Canadians in Canada East were worried. What would happen to them in a separate Canada East with a

> MACDONALD WAS NOT A VISIONARY WHO FOUGHT FOR CAUSES. HE BELIEVED IN GOOD LAWS AND PRACTICAL CHANGES.

French-Canadian majority? But their party—the Liberals—had few members, and was not part of the coalition.

Brown's gesture had broken the deadlock. The idea of a great Confederation had the support of the majority of both French and English Canadians. Its boldness captured their imagination. A union of all the British North American colonies? Let's do it!

But much would depend on whether the three leaders could work together—and stay together. They were very different men with very different goals.

THE LEADERS AND THEIR GOALS

JOHN A. MACDONALD

History is not always fair. Neither is politics.

John A. Macdonald is remembered as the one who did the most to create Canada. Remember, he was the only man honoured by Queen Victoria with a knighthood. He also became the first prime minister of Canada and is pictured on the $10 bill.

However, of the three leaders of the Great Coalition, he was the one who had the least interest in the idea of Confederation!

Macdonald later had great hopes for the future of Canada, but he was not a visionary man; he believed that new ideas often did as much harm as good. Macdonald believed strongly in passing good laws and creating practical changes. But grand ideas were likely to backfire and make things worse. Macdonald was great at organizing and making government work, but he was not a man like George Brown, who could, and did, spend years fighting for his great cause of reform for Canada West.

It was different, though, if Macdonald had no choice but to adopt new ideas. This usually happened when he lost power and had to find a new idea to attract voters. He could also act when faced with a crisis.

> I WAS RIGHT ABOUT PROTECTING FRENCH RIGHTS. MAYBE THERE'D BE NO SEPARATISTS IF YOU'D ALL LISTENED TO ME!
>
> - CHARLES TUPPER

STATE OF THE UNION?

Macdonald supported Confederation in 1864 because it went from being one of Brown's grand, impractical ideas to a political necessity. The Province of Canada was in deadlock. No one, not even Macdonald, could make government work. It was time for something new.

But Macdonald was perhaps our shrewdest and sneakiest leader ever; he also saw a great chance to make sure that he and his party would be able to rule the new Confederation for a long time. As Macdonald saw it, the party that could make the people of Canada West happy by freeing them from Canada East, and could make Canada East's people happy by finding a way to protect their heritage, would win the most votes from both sides.

The Great Coalition would make this possible. Brown and Cartier's support made sure that most members of the assembly would back a government that made Confederation happen. It was a large, secure majority that would let Macdonald get things done. Besides, Macdonald thought, he could separate Brown's party from Brown. Brown was difficult to work with. Macdonald was sure he could charm some of the Reformers if they saw him as a friend instead of as Brown's bitter enemy.

Yes, becoming an avid supporter of Confederation was a very good idea for Macdonald.

GEORGE BROWN

Unlike Macdonald, George Brown was not a natural politician. Brown was a newspaperman. In 1844, he had created the newspaper the *Toronto Globe* (today's *Globe and Mail*) to fight for responsible government, representation by population, and changes to the 1841 union of Canada East and West.

Brown never quite became a good politician. He made mistakes Macdonald would never have made. He made enemies and kept them. He got mad easily. It was all right to get angry with members of other parties, but it was not a good idea to get angry with members of your own, which Brown did regularly. Brown wanted to get things done. If you didn't agree with his ideas, look out! Other Reformers—especially the rouges of Canada East—did not like this. It's hard to work with a leader who doesn't seem to respect you.

Brown was much better at opposing governments than actually governing, because he was such a great journalist. Newspapers in a democracy must be able to criticize the government; they must

watch for government mistakes and tell the people. At the next election, if the people do not like what a government has been doing, they can kick it out.

Brown was always thinking like this. Stop doing bad things! Do good things! Brown was the Reformer who always looked for what was good and bad and told everyone how to make it right. Brown could easily argue for Rep by Pop because he was only interested in the principle. It was the right thing to do, for each man's vote had to be counted equally, which was not happening under the current system. Therefore, Brown was sure it had to be changed.

Macdonald was a better political leader because he could see that what was good for Canada West could be bad for Canada East. Macdonald understood the fears of French Canadians. He was sure that for government to work, it had to do good for all,

> **BROWN MADE MISTAKES THAT MACDONALD NEVER WOULD HAVE MADE.**

not just for a few. So he tried to make a bad system work, even though the bad system was getting worse and worse.

Only when nothing worked could the two men find a way to work together.

GEORGE-ÉTIENNE CARTIER
George-Étienne Cartier had been a rebel all his life—in the name of his people.

He was supposed to have been a descendant of Jacques Cartier, the first French explorer to come to Canada in 1534. Proud of his heritage, he joined the Fils de la liberté in 1837, composed the patriotic song "O Canada, mon pays, mes amours," and fought at Saint-Denis for individual rights against the government of Lower Canada. He was allowed to return to Montreal from exile in 1838 and joined the Saint-Jean-Baptiste Society, which worked to protect French language and heritage. By the time he joined the fight for responsible government, running for a seat in the assembly, he had become a very successful lawyer.

Trusted by all, he rose quickly to become John A. Macdonald's partner in governing the Province of Canada.

With this background, French Canadians knew they could trust Cartier to look out for their interests and rights. While some members of the rouges were upset about the formation of the coalition—one rouge newspaper called Cartier a traitor—most French Canadians were willing to support Cartier and the coalition. They were certain that he would break up the coalition—and stop Confederation—if their rights were attacked.

As long as Cartier supported Confederation, French Canadians would too.

THE ALMOST FORGOTTEN FATHER OF CONFEDERATION

There were other Reformers and Conservatives in both Canadas who would become Fathers of Confederation: Alexander Galt, Hector-Louis Langevin, and poor Thomas D'Arcy McGee, whose sad fate it was to become the only political leader in Canadian history to be assassinated. But there was one other Father of Confederation whose main role in building Confederation came later, after the new country had been born. He is Oliver Mowat, and he did the most to shape the Canada we live in

today. Almost forgotten today, Mowat took on Macdonald in the 1880s—and won.

OLIVER MOWAT

Oliver Mowat and John A. Macdonald began as friends, nearly became partners, and ended as bitter political foes. They were both from Kingston and both served in the government militia against the rebels during the 1837 rebellions. When Mowat decided to become a lawyer, he joined Macdonald's Kingston law office as Macdonald's first law student. (In those days, a law student learned about law from a lawyer, not from a school.) Both were active members of the Kingston Young Men's Debating Society, where they learned to speak so well that they would become great political leaders.

When Mowat became a lawyer in 1841, he was so good that Macdonald wanted him as his partner. But Mowat turned him down. He had done his final studies at a Toronto law firm, where he had a chance to do very well in property law. In years to come, Macdonald would wish that Mowat had become his partner; that way, both of them could not have gone into politics, and Macdonald would not have had to lose to Mowat later in life.

In Toronto, Mowat forged his political views. In 1843, Mowat

met George Brown, and liked him a lot, even if they did not always agree. His family had been Conservative, but Mowat did not want to take a side in politics without thinking carefully about the issues.

BOTH PARTIES WANT MOWAT TO JOIN

In the 1850s, the Conservatives and Reformers both wanted Mowat. He was well-known and would probably win a seat in an election. Mowat thought carefully and decided that he could not join the Conservative government led by Macdonald. He believed that "the ministry would do anything to keep in office; that nothing was too bad in legislation or government to adopt if it would help them to keep their places." Mowat came to believe that the Conservatives had "no higher motive than the love of office with its prestige and its power."

Mowat did not like political parties, but—unlike Brown—realized that a successful political leader needed supporters to win votes and pass good laws. He became a Reformer. Mowat believed that he and Macdonald would no longer be friends but felt that "one must not shape one's political course by friendship."

In 1857, Mowat won a seat in the assembly and soon became

I SAID THE 20TH CENTURY WOULD BELONG TO CANADA. OKAY ... MAYBE THE 21ST!

- WILFRID LAURIER

STATE OF THE UNION?

highly respected. In 1858, just a few months after he won his seat, he was asked to become provincial secretary in George Brown's two-day government but lost his ministry in Macdonald's "double shuffle."

Mowat continued to try to make good laws but became nearly as angry as Brown when legal reforms were made in Canada East, but not in Canada West. When new tariffs were passed that helped businessmen in Canada East but hurt Canada West Mowat had had enough. He worked with Brown to hold a Reform convention in 1859 that proposed a new federation of Canada East and West. The Conservatives laughed at the idea and called it disloyal to the Queen and the empire. Macdonald, though he did not think Confederation was a good idea, said nothing.

MACDONALD TO MOWAT: "YOU DAMNED PUP. I'LL SLAP YOUR CHOPS!"

MOWAT SHOWS UP MACDONALD

Macdonald was not as calm when Mowat convinced the assembly to pass two laws that Macdonald did not like, nor was he happy when Mowat made Macdonald look bad. Macdonald had proposed a law (called a "bill") about bankruptcy that Mowat showed to be bad. Macdonald had to withdraw the proposal.

Macdonald became so angry with Mowat that he nearly hit him in the assembly. The Conservatives and Reformers were all getting angrier with each other as the deadlock intensified. The Conservatives, who thought the Reformers were only making problems worse by wanting changes, sought to show that the Reformers were disloyal.

MACDONALD RETALIATES

In April 1861, Macdonald tried to make Mowat look bad. Macdonald claimed that Mowat, at the Reform convention in 1859, had said that Rep by Pop would be a bad way

CANADA NEEDS TO GET INVOLVED WITH THE WORLD AGAIN. LIKE WE DID IN MY DAY.

- LOUIS ST. LAURENT

STATE OF THE UNION?

to end the political deadlock. This angered Mowat. He insisted that Macdonald had not read the whole line from the speech, which said that federation was "an addition to" Reform party policies, and not a replacement for Rep by Pop. At 1 a.m., he tried to read the whole line to the assembly. Macdonald repeated what he had said. The Speaker then adjourned the meeting.

That didn't end things between Macdonald and Mowat. Macdonald came up to him and waved his hand in Mowat's face while he said, "You damned pup. I'll slap your chops!" The two men were quickly separated.

THE FEUD INTENSIFIES

The feud intensified when Mowat was asked to "redeem" Kingston by taking on Macdonald in his own riding. Then, unlike today, a person could run in more than one riding. Mowat agreed to run against Macdonald.

It was a bitter fight. Macdonald was forced to go door to door to win votes. In the end, he won pretty easily by a margin of 785–474 votes. Mowat won his own seat in Whitby, so the two men would continue to face each other in the assembly.

In 1864, Mowat was asked to join the Great Coalition as postmaster general. He was too popular not to be included. He began to write plans for the new Confederation. Macdonald, who had his own plans for the new country, did not entirely trust him. When the time came, Macdonald would find a way to get Mowat out of the coalition—and hopefully out of politics—so that he could not bother Macdonald anymore.

THE INTERCOLONIAL RAILWAY

If you like railways, the 1840s and 1850s were a great time to be alive. In a time when roads were dirt tracks or made of split logs—and were impossible to travel on in the rain or the snow—railways were the best way to get around.

They were built all over British North America. Cities such as Montreal and Toronto, which were at the centre of the railway networks in the Canadas, grew bigger and bigger. Other cities, seeing the success of Toronto and Montreal, wanted to build more railroads.

They cost a lot to build, however. The Grand Trunk Railway, which connected Sarnia, Canada West, with Montreal, was $4,000,000 in debt when it was completed in 1860. That would be nearly $100,000,000 today. Many railways were started, but not finished, because they cost so much.

The Intercolonial Railway was first proposed in the 1840s. Parts of it were built and opened in Nova Scotia and New Brunswick. In the 1850s, the Grand Trunk Railway was extended from Montreal to Rivière du Loup. However, there were still 800 kilometres of track that had to be built in New Brunswick, as far away as possible from the United States.

In 1862, Britain and the United States had nearly gone to war. Two diplomats from the Confederate States of America, who were going to London, were removed from a British Royal Mail Ship, the RMS *Trent*, by Captain Charles Wilkes of the American warship the USS *San Jacinto*. The United States agreed to release the two diplomats, but the Trent Affair scared people in British North America.

The scare convinced the governments of Nova Scotia, New Brunswick, and Canada that they had to build the Intercolonial Railway so that they could send soldiers to help each other if the United States invaded. Plans for the railway were approved by all three governments in 1862. But the political deadlock in the Province of Canada—and Canadian fears that the cost would be even higher than the cost of building the Grand Trunk Railway—led Canada to drop out in 1863.

The governments of Nova Scotia and New Brunswick were angry. They saw it as proof that the Canadians would not keep their promises. They decided that, if the Canadians could not be trusted, the Maritime colonies might have to join together and create their own union instead.

MONTREAL
200 KM

THE DREAMER WHO DIED FOR CANADA

Thomas D'Arcy McGee's fate was different from that of every other leader who fought for Confederation—he was shot and killed by an assassin.

McGee had begun his political career as a member of George Brown's Reformers. He broke away from the Reformers in 1863 and joined Macdonald's Conservatives. McGee was a powerful defender of minority rights. Born in Ireland, he fought for the rights of the Irish-Catholic minority in the Province of Canada and helped to improve living conditions for Irish immigrants. McGee was able to convince the legislative assembly to create the separate-school system in Ontario.

McGee was one of the first to dream of creating a new nation whose peoples would respect each other's rights. McGee was an eloquent speaker. In an 1860 speech to the legislative assembly, he spoke of his vision for a united British North America:

"I see in the remote distance one great nationality, bound, like the shield of Achilles, by the blue of the ocean. I see it quartered into many communities, each disposing of its own internal affairs, but all bound together by free institutions, free intercourse, free commerce."

McGee fought tirelessly for Confederation. He organized the "leapfrog" tour of the Maritimes in 1864, and helped draft the resolutions at the two 1864 conferences.

However, McGee upset many people in the Irish community because he disliked Fenians. The Fenians were Irish separatists who wanted to take over Canada and trade it back to Britain for a free Ireland (Ireland was a British colony at this time). They wanted Irish men in Canada to revolt at the same time as a Fenian army invaded Canada from the United States.

McGee felt that the Fenians would hurt the Irish reputation in Canada because others would blame all of the Irish for their actions. This is why he spoke out against them. Most Irish people agreed with him and did not join the Fenians. The Fenians never forgave him for this. Even some people in the larger Irish community thought he was a traitor.

In 1867, McGee managed to get elected as a member of Parliament even though many voters hated him. There was a riot when his election was announced. McGee did not become a member of the cabinet, however; in 1868, tired of politics, he asked Macdonald to give him a job in Ottawa.

One night, before McGee started his new job, he was shot and killed as he walked into his home. Patrick James Whelan was hung as McGee's murderer, though there is some doubt even today whether he actually shot McGee.

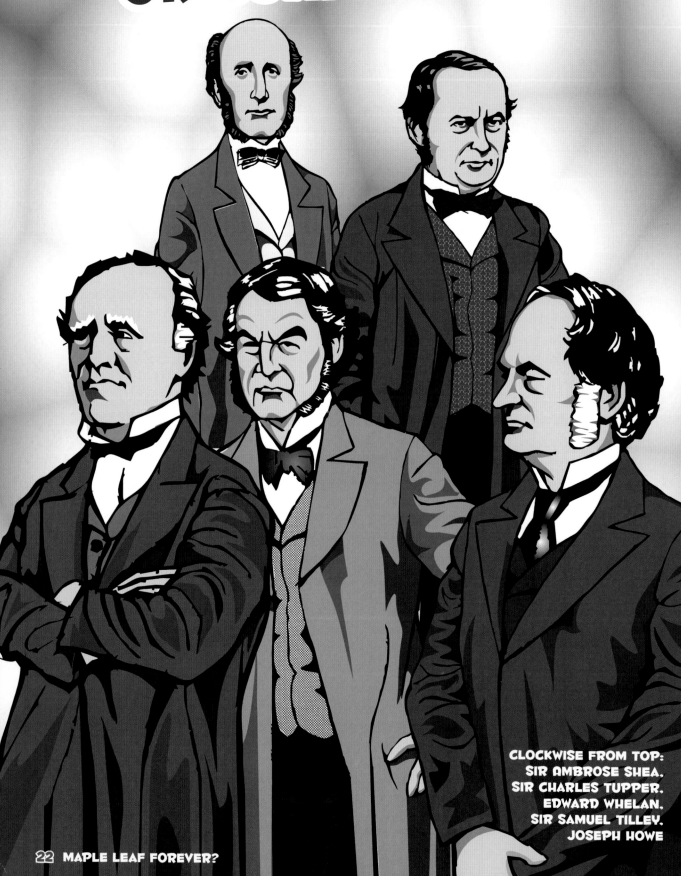

CLOCKWISE FROM TOP:
SIR AMBROSE SHEA,
SIR CHARLES TUPPER,
EDWARD WHELAN,
SIR SAMUEL TILLEY,
JOSEPH HOWE

While the Canadas struggled with political deadlock, the Maritime colonies looked on. The Canadians couldn't do anything right. From politics to managing money to business and trade, the Maritime colonies were simply better. They had achieved responsible government before the Canadians. Except for Newfoundland, they were not in debt and their trading ships could be found in ports all over the world, from Bermuda to India. Who needed the Canadians and their ongoing squabbles?

But they might need each other. Maritime union—in which Nova Scotia, New Brunswick, Prince Edward Island (PEI), and Newfoundland would join together as one colony—might be possible. The United States could be a danger to them all. They might have more power and influence as one big colony instead of four small ones. Could they work together?

Some leaders thought that a confederation of all of Britain's North American colonies might be a good thing. For them, a Maritime union was too small.

NEWFOUNDLAND

Newfoundland had been used by European fishers since the early 1400s and had been visited by Vikings 400 years earlier than that. Newfoundlanders looked east to Britain as much as they looked west to North America. They were proud of their new responsible government and their legislature. Newfoundland's economy was based on fishing and farming. In good times, it prospered, but fishing was poor during the 1860s and fishers caught much less cod than normal. The potato crop was hit by blight and badly damaged. Things were so bad that Governor Anthony Musgrave declared Friday, January 13, 1865, a "day of fasting and humiliation." With times so hard, it was possible that Newfoundland might be interested in Confederation.

> **TOUGH TIMES IN NEWFOUNDLAND IN THE 1860s CONTRIBUTED TO NEWFOUNDLAND'S INTEREST IN CONFEDERATION.**

Newfoundland did not attend the Charlottetown Conference in September 1864; no one there had really thought that they would be involved. But Premier Hugh Hoyles sent two observers to the Quebec Conference in October 1864. One was Ambrose Shea, who thought that Confederation would be good for his colony. However, business leaders such as Charles Fox Bennett did not like Confederation. Bennett owned almost half a million hectares of land and a copper mine and believed strongly that Newfoundland should control its own destiny.

PRINCE EDWARD ISLAND

Before they had been broken up, the other Maritime colonies—today's Nova Scotia, New Brunswick, and PEI—had been one big colony called Nova Scotia.

PEI had been used by King George III to reward military officers and British aristocrats for their loyalty. The island was divided into 67 sections, each 81 square kilometres wide. The new landowners were awarded their sections in a lottery.

The owners were supposed to find settlers to work the land and pay annual quitrents to cover the cost of government. They did neither, however, and the PEI government could not make them do it. People who settled on the land did not own it and could have been kicked off of it by the absentee owners. By the 1860s, both government and farmers in PEI were frustrated; they had been trying to solve the problem for nearly 100 years!

The British government was no help. In the late 1850s, the PEI government had passed laws to force the landowners in Britain to sell the land to the farmers who had settled on it. The British government cancelled the laws, so that they did not have to be obeyed. Only landowners could vote in Britain, and the government would not allow them to be hurt.

In 1864, the Tenant League was created to defend the farmers. It refused to pay rent to the landowners. When sheriffs were sent in to take the land away from the farmers, riots broke out. British troops had to be sent from Halifax to calm things down.

Confederation was worth exploring. Could the new federal government of a united British North America help the people of PEI? Premier John Hamilton Gray supported the idea of Confederation if it would help to solve the land problem. Others, including Edward Whelan, who had helped to pass the laws that Britain had vetoed, did too. Other leaders, such as Attorney General Edward Palmer, were less interested in giving up PEI's self-governing status to a government in Ottawa. They would see what Confederation might offer.

NEW BRUNSWICK

New Brunswick had been created in 1784, after thousands of Loyalists fled the newly formed United States during the American Revolution and settled there. It was too far from Halifax to be governed effectively from that city. Of the four Maritime colonies, New Brunswick was closest to the United States and its leaders wanted to sell more goods, especially lumber, to it. Selling lumber and sailing ships—New Brunswick clipper

ships were among the best ever built—was what made money for the people of the colony.

New Brunswick politics in the 1850s and 1860s was all about railways. Leaders wanted to build a railway joining Saint John to the Maine border to make trade with the United States even easier. Money mattered, not sentiment.

The idea of a British North American Confederation was all right, but if the Province of Canada really wanted to do something for New Brunswick, why not build an Intercolonial Railway to increase trade between New Brunswick and the Canadas?

LEONARD TILLEY

Leonard Tilley, the premier of New Brunswick in 1864, really wanted Confederation to happen. Tilley was not a visionary like Brown or a great speaker and charmer like Macdonald. He had owned a drugstore and been a successful businessman. Tilley had helped to bring responsible government to New Brunswick. He was in favour of reform, including the secret ballot and improved

economic development for New Brunswick. Tilley thought that Confederation would help New Brunswick to get richer. Finally the Intercolonial Railway would be built, bringing more money from the two Canadas. It would give Tilley and New Brunswick money to build the western extension railway line to Maine.

ALBERT SMITH

Albert Smith was New Brunswick's leader of the Opposition. Smith had left Tilley's cabinet in 1862. He wanted to make more reforms than Tilley did and was less interested in helping railway companies with government money. Smith thought that, with a new federal government, New Brunswick would lose control of its local affairs.

NOVA SCOTIA

Nova Scotia was the most successful of the Maritime colonies—and even of all the British North American colonies. Its leaders certainly thought so. Nova Scotia was prosperous. Its builders designed

A PUSH FOR CONFEDERATION

After the Trent Affair and the Intercolonial Railway fiasco, Nova Scotia, New Brunswick, and PEI decided they would try to set up a Maritime union. By the spring of 1864, all three had passed resolutions in their legislatures supporting Maritime

union and suggesting that a conference be held to start planning.

They hadn't gone any further than that; nothing else was ready, and it seemed that the conference might not be held after all, when the Great Coalition was formed

in the Province of Canada. On June 30, the Canadians asked if they could come to the Maritime union conference whenever and wherever it was to be held.

Surprised, the Maritime colonies agreed. They had to hold a conference now!

and built ships that its seamen sailed around the world. Nova Scotia made money through trade with Britain and other British colonies on the Atlantic Ocean.

Halifax was the hub of communications between Britain and the United States. In the days of wooden ships, it was a natural stop for ships sailing across the Atlantic. Halifax was also a major naval port; the Royal Navy's North America and West Indies Squadron was based there. The British Empire was strong and Nova Scotia was a big part of it.

JOSEPH HOWE

Joseph Howe, perhaps the greatest Nova Scotian in history, argued that his fellow citizens "may be pardoned if we prefer London under the dominion of John Bull to Ottawa under the dominion of Jack Frost." Originally a journalist, Howe had entered politics, helped to bring responsible government to Nova Scotia, and had been premier of Nova Scotia from 1860 to 1863. Howe was still a powerful figure in the late 1860s. He was loyal to Nova Scotia, Britain, and the British Empire. Howe saw Nova Scotia as having a big part to play in the growth of the world's greatest empire. Why should Nova Scotians care if the

Canadians couldn't get their act together and make their government work?

But still, a confederation of all of Britain's North American colonies might be good … if there was something in it for Nova Scotia.

CHARLES TUPPER

Charles Tupper thought there would be. Confederation would make Nova Scotia richer and allow it to play a bigger role in the British Empire, which it was too small to do on its own. Nova Scotia would have to join with the other Maritime colonies, or, better yet, with them and the Province of Canada, to create a large country that could do great things. Tupper even went so far as to dream of a "British Amer-

ica, stretching from the Atlantic to the Pacific, [that] would in a few years exhibit to the world a great and powerful organization, with British institutions, British sympathies, and British feelings, bound indissolubly to the throne of England." Tupper shared the same dreams as Macdonald and Brown. No wonder he became friendly with them!

Howe resented Tupper. (He disliked Tupper's idea. He believed that Nova Scotia did not need the Canadas to be great.) The two had long been rivals. Tupper had become a member of the Nova Scotia assembly by beating Howe in an election. Howe saw Tupper as an untalented upstart. He was supposed to have said that "I will not play second fiddle to that damned Tupper!" Howe would watch to see what Tupper did; Tupper could not be allowed to sell out Nova Scotia.

WHICH WAY WOULD THE MARITIMES GO?

MY BILL OF RIGHTS LED TO THE CHARTER OF RIGHTS. BUT I STILL DON'T LIKE THE MAPLE LEAF FLAG.

– JOHN DIEFENBAKER

STATE OF THE UNION?

ONE HOPPING GOOD CONFERENCE

t was pure luck. In August, more than 100 Canadian politicians and newspaper reporters visited Saint John and Halifax. The trip had been set up by Sandford Fleming and Thomas D'Arcy McGee. Fleming wanted to build a railway to join Halifax with the Pacific coast, and McGee wanted to "blast through the ignorance" that kept Canadians and Maritimers from getting to know each other. When Fleming and McGee planned their trip, they had no idea that there was going to be a conference to talk about Confedera-tion only a month later. Their timing was pure luck.

Maritimers did not always trust Canadians. The two Canadas had a bad image in the Maritimes. They'd had rebellions in 1837, railway money scandals in the 1850s, and had pulled out of the Intercolonial Railway deal in 1863. They couldn't run their own government. Hadn't they wangled an invitation to the Charlottetown Conference after their government fell apart and they had to form a coalition? They were in debt, too. Look at how much

WELL, I LOVE MY FLAG! AND I WAS RIGHT – I WAS THE LAST PRIME MINISTER WHO COULD SPEAK ONLY ENGLISH.

– LESTER PEARSON

STATE OF THE UNION?

after a large and hearty lunch, played a game of leapfrog.

But there were also serious speeches—and private talks. In Fredericton, McGee and Tilley each spoke about the possibilities of a union, though Tilley was careful to talk only of customs union, to make it easier to sell the idea among the colonies. In Halifax, old friends McGee and Howe took turns making warm speeches about their colonies. By the end of the tour, the *Halifax Morning Chronicle* said of Howe:

"He was not one of those who thanked God that he was a Nova Scotian merely, for he was a Canadian as well. He had never thought he was a Nova Scotian, but he looked across the broad continent … and studied the mode

by which it could be consolidated … And why should union not be brought about? Was it because we wished to live and die in our insignificance?"

Howe was caught up in the wave of good feelings and said what many Nova Scotians were feeling: they had a big role to play in the world. Where were they to play it?

McGee was happy. The tour had gone well. Many Maritimers—even Howe—were willing to listen to the idea of Confederation.

they owed on the Grand Trunk Railway, for example.

McGee knew that something had to be done to change this image. So, while Macdonald and the others got ready for the conference, McGee took his group on a tour of New Brunswick and Nova Scotia.

And what a tour!

It began August 4 in Saint John, moved to Fredericton, and continued to Halifax. A good time was had by all. The weather was sunny, food was good (and plentiful—people in this era loved to eat), wine flowed freely, speeches were made, and games were played. At the Royal Halifax Golf Club's annual picnic, the Canadians and Maritimers,

CONFERENCE? WHAT CONFERENCE??

By the summer of 1864, the Maritime colonies had flirted with the idea of union, thinking about it but doing nothing else. Then Lord Monck, governor general of the Canadas, wrote to Governor Richard Graves MacDonnell of Nova Scotia, asking if the Canadians could attend.

Surprised, MacDonnell agreed and began to push the others. MacDonnell met with Governor George Dundas of PEI on July 24 and they agreed to hold a conference in Charlottetown, starting September 1. Nova Scotia, New Brunswick, and PEI all chose delegates and the Canadians were hastily invited.

THE CHARLOTTETOWN CONFERENCE

Charlottetown in 1864 was a lovely town of 7,000 people. It was crowded when the conference began: the circus was visiting and there was barely enough room for the delegates in the town's 20 hotels.

The meetings started on September 1 without the Canadians. The Maritime delegates agreed that they would discuss Confederation with the Canadians before they talked any more about Maritime union. It was just as well. They had not really prepared and had no detailed plans.

This was not so with the Canadians, who had spent three days talking about the plans they had written during the summer. Macdonald and Cartier explained how Confederation, with a strong central government, would work. Alexander Galt talked about money and finance: the federal government would pay all the colonies' debts and would give money to the new provinces based on population.

By this time it was Saturday, and the Canadians invited the Maritimers to lunch on their ship, the HMS *Queen Victoria*. They had spent several thousand dollars on food and drink to show the Maritimers a great time. As they enjoyed the food and champagne, everyone relaxed and talk turned to the future. Cartier and Brown talked of a new nation that would stretch from the Atlantic to the Pacific.

The party went well into the next day and the dream took hold. Canadians, Nova Scotians, and New Brunswickers all saw a greater role for themselves in the

PRE-CONFERENCE FUN AT THE CIRCUS!

THE DREAM TAKES HOLD

George Brown sealed the deal. He explained how the new country would work. There would be two levels of government. One, the federal government, would run the country. The colonies would become provinces and would run the local governments. The two Canadas would be split into two separate provinces. The different levels of government would have control over different things. The federal government would run the police and army, which had to be the same everywhere. Provincial governments would run schools and hospitals. These responsibilities would be called the "powers" of each government.

British Empire and the world. A new country—one of the largest on earth—would become a great country. Why not go for it? Why not build it?

When the Canadians finished their presentations, the Maritime delegates were impressed.

DISAGREEMENT SETS IN

They met by themselves on Wednesday, September 7, to discuss Maritime union. Charles Tupper suggested that they create a union of Nova Scotia, New Brunswick, and PEI. But he had no plans for how this would work. Where would the capital

of the union be? Each colony had very different schools; how could they be combined into one system?

The discussion quickly became insulting. New Brunswick's delegates did not want the capital in Halifax and said that the location of the capital would be a problem. They then insulted PEI by saying it would be a good thing for it to become a "partner in the land of New Brunswick." PEI's Premier Gray angrily answered that "the disadvantages to the island would be great" if PEI joined a Maritime union.

MARITIME UNION? NOT!

It was quickly clear that the idea was dead. Leonard Tilley asked a simple question: why not get Confederation going, and then—if anyone really wanted to—form the Maritime union? Everyone thought this was a good idea.

The Canadians were asked to rejoin the meeting and the Maritime delegates all agreed—as George Brown recalled later—that Confederation was "highly

desirable, if the terms of union could be made satisfactory." Happy, the Canadians invited the Maritime delegates to a meeting in Quebec to discuss the final terms.

The conference went on—but now it was fun time! On September 8, a party began at 10 a.m., with supper not served until after midnight. The leaders became better friends, dining, drinking, and dancing with the elegant wives and daughters of Charlottetown society until dawn, when the group boarded the *Queen Victoria* and set sail for Nova Scotia.

The Canadians and Maritimers partied in Nova Scotia and New Brunswick for the next few days, learning to trust each other. Many became close friends. Tupper at this time grew close to Macdonald and Cartier. Macdonald was impressed by Tupper. He later said that, on the first day of the conference, he realized that Tupper was essential if Confederation was to work. These friendships became important later, when Confederation ran into trouble and figures such as Howe did their best to block it.

THE CHARLOTTETOWN CONFERENCE DELEGATES

PROMISES, PROMISES

Between and during the parties, talk continued about the terms of Confederation. George Coles of PEI said that the delegates agreed that the island would get £200,000 ($1,000,000 at the time, or about $15,000,000 today)—or the interest earned on that money—to buy land for PEI's farmers from the absentee landlords.

The fun times finally ended in mid-September—and not because the delegates had run out of food and drink. There was a lot of work to be done for the Quebec Conference and only three weeks until it began.

QUEBEC CONFERENCE

In the fall of 1864, Quebec City was the capital of the Province of Canada. Then, as now, it was a beautiful city. The visitors from the Maritimes were much impressed. They were joined by delegates from Newfoundland, who now wanted to participate.

The conference began on Monday, October 10, and continued until October 28. The meetings

were long. The delegates would meet from 10 a.m. to 2 p.m., take a recess, and meet again from 7:30 p.m. until early morning. The recesses were busy, as delegates spent time writing and talking, trying to convince each other to accept or reject a new idea.

PROPOSED FEDERAL STRUCTURE

The federal government would be made up of two houses: the House of Commons and the Senate. House of Commons members would be elected by the votes of the people. Senate members would be chosen by the prime minister. The Senate would have to obey the elected House of Commons if there was disagreement because the power to rule in Canada comes from the people. Both the federal and the provincial governments were to be based on the principle of responsible government. The federal House of Commons and the provincial legislative assemblies would work in the same way that the colonies' legislative assemblies did. The federal government was given strong powers. It would control trade and commerce, foreign affairs, finance, and criminal law. It would be able to put tariffs on things that were made in the United States or Britain; people would have to pay more money for those things, but the money would go to the federal government, which would then give some of this money to the provinces. It was even given the power to *disallow*, or cancel, any provincial law. The federal government would also be given any powers not included in the list of provincial powers. It would be very, very strong.

PARTY TIME … AGAIN

As in Charlottetown, there were many parties before and after the formal meetings. After the conference ended, the hotel bills came to $15,000 ($225,000 today). Despite the church's best efforts to stop "intimate dancing," Canadian delegates spent a lot of time dancing with the

wives and daughters of the Maritimers. Edward Whelan of PEI noted: "They are cunning fellows; and there's no doubt that it is all done for a political purpose; they know that if they can dance themselves into the affections of the wives and daughters of the country, the men will certainly become an easy conquest." Macdonald even went so far as to visit Mercy Coles, the daughter of PEI delegate George Coles, who was very sick and confined to her hotel room. Miss Coles liked Macdonald and enjoyed his visits. Even so, she knew that Macdonald was trying to reach her father, who had begun to think Confederation was a bad idea.

Coles was not the only person at the Quebec Conference who was changing his mind. Charlottetown had been fun, but now that it came time to work out the details, they did not always agree.

PEI BECOMES UPSET

PEI's delegates were the first to become upset. They did not like being controlled by the Canadians, who were presenting written drafts of the details to the Maritimers. The Maritimers didn't present their own ideas very often.

Nor did PEI like the details the Canadians were presenting.

The Canadians wanted the number of seats each province had in the new House of Commons to be based on its population—this was Rep by Pop. It would give PEI five seats in the House, but PEI wanted six. The Canadians said no.

The Canadians then decided not to give PEI money to buy land for farmers—money that PEI thought had been promised at Charlottetown. Angry, the PEI delegates turned to their fellow Maritimers for the promised $150,000. New Brunswick was promised $63,000 per year, but Tupper decided not to ask for any money for Nova Scotia. The Canadians had also agreed to make sure the Intercolonial Railway was finally built. The

SICK AND CONFINED TO BED 16-YEAR-OLD MERCY KEEPS A DIARY ABOUT THE SUMMER CONFERENCES. MACDONALD VISITS HER HOPING TO WIN HER FATHER'S SUPPORT.

other Maritime delegates agreed with the Canadians.

George Coles was shocked. He knew this would end any chance of PEI joining Confederation, for the people of PEI would not see any benefit.

The conference also had to decide what powers each level of government would have. Oliver Mowat, who had not been at Charlottetown, helped to write the lists of powers and introduced them for discussion.

Macdonald really wanted to have only one government for Canada and to get rid of the provincial governments. But Cartier told him that French Canada would not accept this. Tupper said the same about Nova Scotia and New Brunswick, which did not want to be "swamped" by Canada West. There had to be

local, provincial governments.

Macdonald accepted that. But he wanted the provincial governments to be weak. He thought that the United States Civil War had begun because the states were too strong and could stand up to the federal government. He did not want that to happen in Confederation. So he made sure that the federal government was able to decide how much money each province would get and that it could cancel provincial law. Macdonald was sure that, in time, the provincial governments would be taken over by "the general power" (the federal government)—though he only said this in a private letter to M. C. Cameron, a fellow Conservative member of the Canadian legislative assembly.

Mowat did not argue with Macdonald at Quebec. But he was as good a lawyer as Macdonald, if not better. The powers that he helped to give to the provincial governments were also important. They ran schools, health care, and prisons. They were given power over "property and civil rights." This has nothing to do with human rights; it deals with who owns property, businesses, and contracts. Finally, the provinces were given power over "generally all matters of a private or local nature," which could change or grow in time.

Macdonald worked with Mowat to write the lists of powers

but did not really trust him. Then he saw a chance to get Mowat out of politics. One of the three judges of the Court of Chancery

> **MACDONALD WAS SURE THAT, IN TIME, THE PROVINCIAL GOVERNMENTS WOULD BE TAKEN OVER BY THE FEDERAL GOVERNMENT – BUT HE WOULDN'T SAY SO OPENLY.**

of the Province of Canada died while the Quebec Conference was going on. Macdonald offered the judgeship—a job for life—to Mowat. This was an important job that Mowat could not refuse, but it meant he would have to leave politics. A judge must be fair to everyone and cannot be involved in politics. So Mowat, who was both tired of politics and honoured by the offer, took

the job. Macdonald was happy to see him go; it meant that Macdonald could be sure that his plan for a strong federal and weak provincial governments would be accepted. It was.

The conference ended on October 28, when the delegates approved the final version of the Quebec Resolutions—the rules of Confederation.

Now each colony had to approve the terms. Would they find them satisfactory, as had been agreed at Charlottetown? Or would Confederation be defeated?

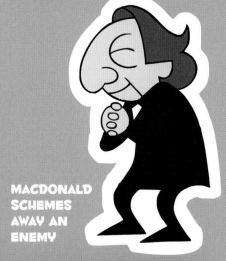

MACDONALD SCHEMES AWAY AN ENEMY

ROBERT HARRIS'S FAMOUS PAINTING OF FATHERS OF CONFEDERATION

CONFEDERATION DEFEATED

WITH THE PARTIES OVER, THE FIGHTING BEGINS

Even though the Quebec Resolutions had been accepted by all delegates, they needed to be approved by each colony for Britain to pass the law that would make Confederation happen.

THE APPROVAL PROCESS

Approval could happen in one of two ways. A general election could be held, and if the voters elected a government that wanted Confederation, it would hold a vote in the legislative assembly to approve the Quebec Resolutions. The government would then go ahead and join Confederation.

The other way was for the government to debate the resolutions. A vote would be held after the debate and if a majority voted in favour, the government could join Confederation.

After the Quebec Conference ended, Macdonald and others hoped that it would not take long for each colony's government to agree to join. If all went well, maybe the new country could be born in 1865.

It took a lot longer than that. Not everyone liked the idea of Confederation—it was now their turn to take part in the debate.

NEWFOUNDLAND'S DECISION

Because Newfoundlanders were proud of their colony and didn't like pressure from anyone, the Newfoundland legislative assembly did not debate Confederation until February 1865. The people who didn't like Confederation were very critical.

Store owners in St. John's did not want to join at all. They were sure that the new federal government would put tariffs on things that they bought from Britain or the United States. This meant that they would have to raise prices and lose both business and money. If it was going to cost them, there was no way they wanted any part of Confederation.

Others said that there were nearly 1,000 kilometres of sea between Newfoundland and the other colonies. People had close ties to Britain, not North America. Confederation might be a good idea in principle for the other colonies, but it was not a good idea for them.

The fishers in the towns and villages on Newfoundland's coasts were conservative and did not really like the idea of change. Proud and tough, they preferred to go on as they were and not be seen as needing outside help.

Even pressure from Britain—through Governor Sir Anthony Musgrave—didn't work. Newfoundlanders simply did not want to be pushed. Knowing this, the Newfoundland government decided not even to call a vote on the issue. Newfound-landers would wait and see what happened.

PRINCE EDWARD ISLAND'S DECISION

George Coles had left Quebec feeling sure that the people of PEI would not join Confederation. He turned out to be right.

In February 1865, the Quebec Resolutions were presented to the PEI assembly to consider. As in Newfoundland, people had a lot of reasons not to join.

> **NOT EVERYONE LIKED CONFEDERATION – IT WAS NOW THEIR TURN TO TAKE PART IN THE DEBATE**

PEI was also an island. It was able to grow enough food to feed its people. Most Islanders had never left PEI and saw no reason to. Why leave the best place in the world?

Instead, people thought that PEI could only be hurt if it joined Confederation. Store owners could only be hurt by tariffs, just as in Newfoundland. The new federal government would use the tariff money—and probably other taxes too—to pay to build the Intercolonial Railway—but what good would that do PEI? The railway would never reach the island. Even worse, boys and men in PEI might be forced to go to Canada West to fight the Americans. But PEI had no border with the Americans, so why should they fight?

Edward Whelan and George Coles tried to say that if the other colonies got richer, it would help PEI—and the Americans might want PEI if they took over the rest of the colonies. But there were two arguments against joining Confederation that even they had to agree with.

The Islanders were upset about Rep by Pop. They said that it was unfair to PEI. Why should the city of Montreal have more seats in the new House of Commons than the province of PEI? This would mean that the federal government would pay more attention to the people of Montreal than to the people of PEI.

The Islanders' big problem was the absentee landlords in Britain. If the new federal government was not going to spend the money to help the farmers of PEI—and most Islanders were farmers—what good was it?

In May 1866, the PEI assembly voted for a resolution that said "any federal union of the North American colonies that would embrace this island would be

I BROUGHT THE CONSTITUTION HOME. AND EVERY PROVINCE ACCEPTED IT – EVEN QUEBEC. TO THOSE WHO THINK IT DIDN'T – FUDDLE DUDDLE!

– PIERRE TRUDEAU

STATE OF THE UNION?

hostile to the feelings and the wishes as it would be opposed to the best and most vital interests of its people." In October 1866, Tilley and Tupper made an offer of $800,000 to buy out the land-owners, but it was too late.

PEI said no to Confederation.

NEW BRUNSWICK'S DECISION

In New Brunswick as well, numerous people did not want Confederation, many of them members of Tilley's government. Unlike today, when a premier or prime minister can tell the members of his party what to do, premiers in the 1800s were not strong enough to force their members to vote for anything. The only way to make them vote for Confederation was to have a general election.

If the people voted for members of the assembly who wanted to join Confederation, Tilley could then persuade those who did not want Confederation to vote for it anyway. So Tilley called an election for March 1865.

Unfortunately for Tilley, his plan didn't work. He and his party lost the election. Only 11 of the 41-member assembly wanted to join Confederation.

NOVA SCOTIA'S DECISION

Charles Tupper was sure that he would have no trouble getting the Nova Scotia legislative assembly to vote to join Confederation. His party had the most seats in the assembly. Even better, opposition leaders also wanted Confederation.

Tupper had forgotten about Joseph Howe, who was opposed to joining.

Howe did not want Nova Scotia to give up its power—and its right—to rule itself. He was sure that the two Canadas, especially Canada West, would have the most seats in the new House of Commons. Under responsible government, the House of Commons would pay more attention to the voters from the two Canadas. Why, Howe asked, would Nova Scotians want to join a Confederation in which the federal government did not pay attention to their needs, when they already had a government that did a good job?

Howe also reminded Nova Scotians of their pride. It was a good idea to make all the colonies one country, Howe said, but Confederation was not the way to do it. It gave too much to the two Canadas, and not enough to Nova Scotia.

Others thought Howe was right. Tupper had not asked for any money from the new federal government, the way that New Brunswick and Newfoundland had. Many business people thought that Nova Scotia would go bankrupt if it joined Confederation.

Tupper was getting ready to fight back. Then New Brunswick held its election and voted not to join Confederation. Tupper saw that the members of his party had changed their minds. Like Tilley, Tupper could not tell his party members how to vote. But Tupper knew that if he called a general election, the voters would elect members opposed to joining.

Tupper thought about what he should do. People who had wanted to vote for Confederation had changed their minds once. They might do so again. In April 1865, Tupper said that "12 months will, I believe, find a decided majority in the present parliament in favour of Confederation." Tupper decided to wait. He would not ask the assembly to decide—yet.

TIILLEY: "IS ALL LOST?"

THE PROVINCE OF CANADA'S DECISION

There was never any doubt about the Canadian assembly's decision. The leaders of the Great Coalition all wanted Confederation.

They really did not have much choice; there was no turning back. The old system did not work. There had to be a new form of government to replace it. However, some people did think that there should be a general election to let voters have their say. Macdonald, Brown, and Cartier didn't think this was a good idea. This was, after all, responsible government. It was the duty of members of the legislative assembly to make these decisions. And if the voters didn't like a decision, they could always kick the members out of office in the next election.

Besides, the voters knew all about Confederation. The newspapers—and there were a lot of them in 1865!—had written all about it. Most members of the assembly supported it; three of the four parties in the assembly would vote in favour. The party that did not want to join—the rouges—was small and could not win enough seats in a general election to stop Confederation.

> ### THE PROVINCE OF CANADA REALLY HAD NO CHOICE BECAUSE THE OLD SYSTEM HAD BROKEN DOWN.

Still, some people, especially in Canada East, did not really want to join. The rouges thought Confederation, with its strong federal government, would hurt French-Canadian rights. They were also concerned about the federal government's power to disallow provincial laws. The bleus, led by Cartier, were sure that French-Canadian ministers would be able to protect their people. Most French Canadians trusted Cartier.

So, on March 15, 1865, the assembly voted on the government motion that the Canadas should join Confederation. Even news that New Brunswick had voted against it did not change the outcome: Confederation won 91–33. Canada West voted 57–8 in favour; Canada East's members supported it by a vote of 34–25.

CONFEDERATION DEFEATED?

By March 1865, only the Province of Canada had decided to join Confederation. Would any other colony want to join? It didn't look like it, even though Macdonald and Tupper were willing to wait for events. Only outside forces might convince people to change their minds.

In April 1865, the US Civil War ended. The United States now had a very large army that had nothing to do.

Would it be sent north to take over British North America?

There were some in the United States who thought this was an excellent idea.

THE MARITIMES SAY NO!

UNEASY NEIGHBOURS

After the Seven Years' War, Great Britain had taken over all of North America east of the Mississippi River. The British already had colonies on the east coast of North America; now they owned New France, which had belonged to France, as well.

The British decided that their colonies would have to help pay for the Seven Years' War, which had been fought all over the world. Some historians consider it to be the first world war. The British colonists in America did not want this. After all, the war was over and they were safe from attack. Besides, they had helped the British to fight the French in New France. Now Britain wanted them to pay?

THE US IS CREATED

This argument led to the American Revolution in 1776. The British colonies on the east coast of North America broke away from Britain to form their own country, the United States of America.

> **BRITISH NORTH AMERICA AND THE USA DID NOT REALLY TRUST EACH OTHER.**

Many people who lived in the United States did not want to live there anymore and fled north to Nova Scotia, New Brunswick, and Canada West. They were called Loyalists and they wanted to live in British colonies.

But there were also many Americans who really disliked the British. In 1812, the United States and Britain were at war over the colonies. While this ended in a tie, it created a sense of pride in the British North American colonists, who had held off the much larger United States.

After the War of 1812, Great Britain and the United States made agreements, called "treaties," which made them less likely to fight another war. One of those treaties, the Rush-Bagot Agreement of 1817, limited each side to four military ships on the Great Lakes. Both countries still obey this treaty today! Over the next 30 years, treaties were agreed to that clearly marked the borders between the British colonies and the United States.

Still, the two did not really trust each other. Worried the United States might attack them again, the colonies tried to move railways away from the American border, so that they could not be captured easily.

WHAT IF?

THE SOUTH HAD WON THE CIVIL WAR?

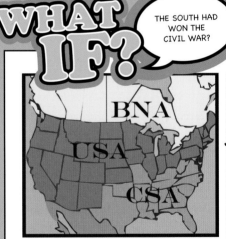

THE NORTHERN ARMY LOSES THE BATTLE OF GETTYSBURG IN 1862 (WHICH IT WON IN ACTUAL HISTORY, ALLOWING THE NORTH TO KEEP FIGHTING). PRESIDENT LINCOLN MUST ADMIT THE CIVIL WAR IS OVER; THE USA HAS LOST.

TODAY, JANUARY 1ST, 1863, WE RECOGNIZE THE **CONFEDERATE STATES OF AMERICA** AS A NEW NATION, SEPARATE FROM THE UNITED STATES.

AFRAID THAT BRITAIN WILL HELP THE **CSA** BY ATTACKING FROM CANADA, THE **USA** PUTS A STRONG ARMY AND NAVY ON THE BORDER. TRADE IS REDUCED TO LIMIT VISITORS FROM CANADA, WHO COULD BE **CSA** SPIES.

IN 1866, THE UNITED STATES CONGRESS OFFERS THE BRITISH NORTH AMERICA COLONIES MONEY, INVESTMENTS IN BETTER RAILWAYS, AND AGREES TO PAY ANY DEBTS THE COLONIES OWE IF THEY JOIN THE UNITED STATES.

1866 AN INVITATION TO CANADA TO JOIN THE UNITED STATES

SURELY YOU CAN DEFEND US FROM THE **USA**!

NOT AGAINST A TWO MILLION MAN ARMY. YOU ARE ON YOUR OWN.

UNABLE TO REFUSE, CANADA JOINS THE **USA** ON JULY 1ST, 1867. PRESIDENT LINCOLN ABOLISHES SLAVERY AND DECLARES A "FREE NATION", UNLIKE THE **CSA**, WHICH ALLOWS SLAVERY.

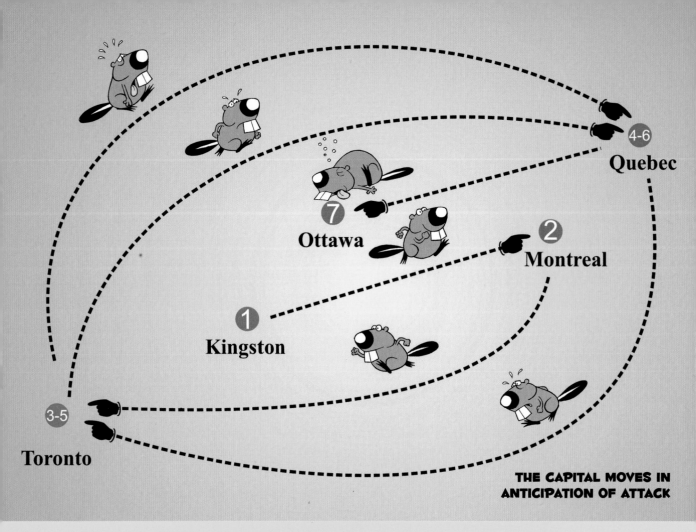

Map illustration with labeled cities: Quebec (4-6), Montreal (2), Ottawa (7), Kingston (1), Toronto (3-5), with dashed lines connecting them and cartoon beavers carrying items.

Quebec 4-6

Ottawa 7

Montreal 2

Kingston 1

Toronto 3-5

THE CAPITAL MOVES IN ANTICIPATION OF ATTACK

In 1857, the Province of Canada moved its capital from Kingston to Ottawa (it had been in both Montreal and Toronto), so that it would be farther away from the border in case the United States attacked.

RECIPROCITY TREATY

In 1854, the two sides agreed to a treaty that made it easier for the colonies and the United States to trade with each other. The Reciprocity Treaty of 1854 lowered the tariffs that had to be paid when the Americans or the British sold something to the other country that they'd mined or grown. This meant that the tariff would not be added and items from across the border would not cost as

much. The treaty lasted until 1866, when the Americans cancelled it. They did not think it was helping Americans to sell things in the British colonies.

THE UNITED STATES CIVIL WAR

Americans were also upset with the British and their North American colonies because of the US Civil War. The United States had become divided. The northern states, also called the North, were industrialized; people worked in factories as well as on farms. In the southern states, or the South, people made their living by farming. Many of the farms were run by whites, but slaves—people who had been brought from Africa,

and their children—actually did the work.

Bringing new slaves into Upper Canada was banned in 1793. Children born into slavery were freed at age 25. Eventually, the practice died out there. However, the United States didn't stop bringing in new slaves from Africa until 1808. And its government did not end slavery for slaves and their children already living in the United States.

All northern states abolished slavery between 1780 and 1804. They tried to stop it in the South too, but Southerners fought to keep it. As the United States grew, there were bitter fights about allowing slavery in the new states of the West.

The two sides agreed to allow slavery below a marker called

the Mason-Dixon Line. States south of the line were slave states; those to the north were free states. However, this did not stop the fights.

The northern states and some new Midwestern states disliked slavery, and were worried that slave owners in the South were gaining power in the national government. The Republican party was created in 1854 to stop slavery.

CONFEDERACY FORMS

In 1860, the Republicans chose Abraham Lincoln to run for president. After he won the election, seven southern states decided to leave the United States and form their own country, which they called the Confederate States of America, or the Confederacy. Four other states joined the Confederacy in April 1861, after Lincoln became president.

Lincoln felt he couldn't allow the southern states to leave. Nothing in the United States constitution allowed this. For Lincoln, his country was "one nation, indivisible." However, the Confederacy struck the first blow, attacking the North at Fort Sumter, North Carolina.

EMANCIPATION PROCLAMATION

Lincoln thought slavery was wrong and in 1863 issued the Emancipation Proclamation, which accelerated the end of slavery in the United States. Lincoln believed that the only way to rebuild after the war was to take away the issue that had led to war in the first place.

ISSUED BY US PRESIDENT LINCOLN IN 1863, THIS DECREE BEGINS THE PROCESS OF ENDING SLAVERY IN THE SOUTHERN STATES

Still, the only way to make sure that the United States would be reunited into one country, and to end slavery, was to win the war with the Confederacy. Lincoln and his generals built a strong Union army of over two million men. Still it took until 1865 to defeat the South.

BNA AND THE UNITED STATES CIVIL WAR

Great Britain and its colonies decided to remain neutral. But some incidents nearly led to war between the United States and Britain.

Remember the Trent Affair? It led both the Canadas and Nova Scotia to add more men to their militias—men who would protect them if they were attacked. Britain made plans to defend British North America, sending 18,000 officers and men to the colonies. They expected to face an invasion force of 50,000 to 200,000 American soldiers. They also prepared to attack the North. Fortunately, President Lincoln realized he could not fight both Britain and the South and reached an agreement with Britain. But both Britain and the colonies were scared by how close they had come to war. What might happen after the North defeated the South?

After the Emancipation Proclamation of 1863, people in Britain and the colonies wanted the North to win. However, the South used the Province of Canada as a base to attack the United States, creating problems for everyone.

In October 1864, Lieutenant Bennett H. Young of the Confederate army led 21 men in a raid on St. Albans, Vermont, where they stole $208,000 (over $3,000,000 today) and tried to burn down the town. When they returned to Canadian territory, they were arrested. The North was angry and wanted the raiders sent to Vermont to be punished. However, a court decided that since Canada was neutral, and the raiders were soldiers obeying orders, it could not return them. Only the money was returned.

THE FENIAN RAIDS

After the civil war ended, the United States no longer needed a large army and many of the soldiers were allowed to leave. They could take their guns with them if they paid $6 ($70 today). Many did and went looking for another battle to fight.

They found it with the Fenians.

The Fenians were formed in 1858. They had come from Ireland to the United States and wanted to free Ireland from Britain. There were many Irish in the northern United States who thought this a good idea.

Macdonald and Joseph Howe were worried about the Fenians, seeing them as a threat to attack the colonies. They grew more worried when they learned that many men who had been soldiers in the Union army—men who already had guns—were joining the Fenians.

> **THE FENIANS WANTED TO CAPTURE CANADA AND TRADE IT FOR IRELAND'S FREEDOM.**

In March 1866, both Canada and Nova Scotia readied their militias to fight the Fenians. The British sent soldiers and ships across the Atlantic to protect the Nova Scotia coast. Nothing happened until April, when 500 Fenians met in Eastport, Maine, close to the border of New Brunswick.

FENIANS ATTACK NB

On April 14, 1866, five Fenians attacked Indian Island in the St. Croix River, putting their guns to the head of the deputy customs collector and stealing the British flag. The British sent more soldiers and ships to protect the river.

The United States government decided that it would not help the Fenians, even though some Americans in New York were in favour. Instead, it sent General Meade with 300 troops aboard the USS Regulator to help the British, who had sent the HMS Duncan from Halifax with 700 troops, stop the Fenians.

The Fenians had no chance. They gave up their attack on New Brunswick. The American army captured 1,500 rifles and 100,000 bullets in Eastport.

The Fenians did not give up entirely. On May 31, 1,500 Fenians attacked Canada West. They arrived in Fort Erie on June 1 and fought some Canadian volunteers in Ridgeway the following day, killing six Canadians and wounding 30.

The Fenians returned to the United States when no more soldiers joined them. The American government arrested 400 of the attackers.

On June 7, 1,300 Fenians attacked Canada East and set up a camp at Pigeon Hill. American president Johnson said that the United States would not help the Fenians, who returned to the country on June 11 to find that General Meade had captured their guns and supplies.

The British and the Canadians were happy that the Ameri-

I WISH IT HAD BEEN MORE THAN A SUMMER JOB [SIGH] ...

- JOHN TURNER

STATE OF THE UNION?

cans had helped them to defeat the Fenians, but were not pleased that they had to rely on the Americans to stop the Fenian attacks. They needed to make their defences stronger. What if the United States didn't help them during future raids?

A WARNING ABOUT THE FUTURE

This was a problem. Some Americans clearly wanted to take over British North America. On July 2, 1866, a member of the United States congress—their version of the legislative assembly—suggested that the British colonies join the United States. General N. P. Banks wanted congress to write a law that described how the British colonies could join the United States. Congress ignored Banks's suggested law, but still it made British North Americans angry—it was a warning about the future. Could they always count on American goodwill to leave them alone—or could they do something to help themselves?

Canada East

Canada West

New Brunswick

Indian Island

Pigeon Hill

Nova Scotia

Ridgeway

United States of America

Fenian Raids on the British Colonies in North America

ATTACK FROM THE SOUTH

CHARLES PULLS IT OFF - WITH A LITTLE HELP FROM THE FENIANS

NOVA SCOTIA CHANGES ITS MIND

On April 10, 1866, in Nova Scotia, Charles Tupper presented a motion to the legislative assembly urging that a way be found to create a union to protect Nova Scotia's interests.

After several days of debate—and after the Fenian attack on Indian Island on April 14—the legislative assembly voted 31–19 in favour of Tupper's motion. Nova Scotia's assembly had agreed to join Confederation.

Still, people who didn't want to join Confederation were not happy. They believed that Tupper had used fear of the Fenians to make the assembly approve Confederation.

Others asked why Tupper hadn't called an election to let the people decide. This was an important decision about the future, they said. Shouldn't the people decide?

Tupper replied in the same way as Macdonald and Cartier had: this was responsible government. The members who had been elected to the assembly had the ability to make this decision. If they thought they could not make it, they could vote against Tupper's motion, forcing Tupper to call an election. Since the assembly had voted in favour of Confederation, Tupper said, there was no need for an election.

Tupper has been criticized for this decision ever since. Confederation was a major change in the way that Nova Scotians lived. Many at the time, supported by many historians since 1866, believed that Tupper should have asked the people.

When Nova Scotians did get a chance to vote, they would make their feelings about how Tupper had handled the situation very clear.

NEW BRUNSWICK CHANGES ITS MIND

After the 1865 election, New Brunswick's premier was Albert Smith. Soon, Smith found that his party members could not agree on what laws to make. The only thing they could agree on was that they did not like Confederation.

Smith had changed his mind about the union of the North American colonies; he now believed it was a good idea. But he thought that the plan for Confederation was not good for New Brunswick. Then Smith changed his mind again. He said his government had no plan for any form of union at all.

On April 10, 1866, Smith had to resign as premier, as no one knew what his policy on union of the colonies was. An election was called for June 1866. Tilley and Smith both knew that Confederation would be the big issue.

Both sides needed money to fight the election—and both sides got it. Historians think that the 1866 election was corrupt: many voters were paid for

> **IN THE NEW BRUNSWICK ELECTION OF 1866 BOTH SIDES OFFERED $120 (IN TODAY'S MONEY) PER VOTE.**

their support. Smith got thousands of dollars from people in Halifax who wanted to stop Confederation. Tilley, meanwhile, wrote to Macdonald, telling him that the election could be won if he got "thousands of dollars" of "the needful." Both sides offered $10 ($120 in today's money) per vote!

While many voters liked the money, many more New Brunswickers were alarmed about the dangers from the United States and the Fenians. In June, they elected 31 members to the assembly who would vote to join Confederation. Smith was only able to elect eight members who were opposed.

Tilley quickly called a meeting of the legislative assembly.

On June 25, New Brunswick's assembly voted 31–8 to join.

Tilley had been right when he'd said, a year before, that the people of New Brunswick would change their minds in 12 months.

CANADA EAST AND THE FENIAN RAIDS

The raids also helped to convince many people in Canada East to support Confederation. The successful raid on Pigeon Hill made it clear that the United States could be a danger in the future and that it was best for all of the colonies to work together to meet the threat.

With approval from four colonies, it was time to go to London, England. The British parliament would have to pass a law to make Confederation happen, although it had to be written by the British North Americans themselves. It took time for everyone to get ready to go, so the meeting did not begin in London until December 1866.

When the delegates arrived, they found that Joseph Howe was already there. This was Howe's last chance. Could he convince the British to stop Confederation?

CONFEDERATION TRIUMPHANT

Joseph Howe went to London, England, in June 1866. The British were his last chance to stop Confederation. Howe was sure that the British could tell Macdonald, Tupper, and the others either to stop Confederation or to change its terms. Britain ruled the world's greatest empire, after all—surely it could tell its colonial political leaders what to do.

The British had been thinking about the idea of uniting all of its North American colonies for a long time. There was no hurry.

However, the US Civil War changed their plans. Prior to this, the British did not feel that it was too difficult to defend their North American colonies. In the War of 1812, a small number of British soldiers, with the help of British North American militias and First Nations peoples, were able to hold off the United States. Most of the American forces had been militia, who would fight to defend their country but would not cross the border to attack British North America. The United States army itself was not very big. The civil war changed everything.

For the first time, the United States had built a large formal army. But after the war—and it was obvious by 1865 that the North would win—it was not clear what the United States would do with that army. There were signs its leaders might choose to turn north and attack British North America.

Great Britain's power was based on its Royal Navy—the largest in the world—and not its army. The British knew that they did not have enough soldiers to fight the new, large American army. Yet they could not sit by and do nothing if the Americans attacked.

The colonies would have to help, just as the British had expected the American colonies to help out in the 1770s. But the British had learned from their mistakes. This time, they thought it would be better if the colonies united to defend themselves. The United States would not be able to pick off each colony one by one.

Great Britain also had to look out for its own interests. The British were worried about the rise of Germany and Italy, which had become large, united countries for the first time in the 1860s. They might be a threat to Great Britain and its empire. With problems closer to home, Great Britain did not want to fight the United States if it did not have to.

Besides, the British and Americans had been good trading part-

either the colonies or the United States. The British wanted a union of the British North American colonies to happen, but they did not want the reasons for Confederation to be known. They did not want to look weak in the eyes of the Americans or the Europeans, both of whom sometimes resented the power of the British Empire.

GREAT BRITAIN AND CONFEDERATION

When the Confederation plan began in the Province of Canada, Great Britain was pleased and wanted to do what it could to make it happen.

The British Colonial Office in London was responsible for running the colonies. The colonial secretary, the member of the British cabinet who ran the Colonial Office, thought that this would be easy. They would simply order the governor of each colony to tell the colonial governments what to do.

This didn't work. The governments of the colonies thought that it was up to them—and their legislative assemblies—to decide whether or not to join Confederation. The governors found that they could not just

ners and trade would grow again now that the civil war was over. Under the Monroe Doctrine, Great Britain and the United States had even worked together

to keep other European countries from setting up their own colonies in North and South America.

So the British found that they had to be careful not to anger

tell the colonists what to do. For example, in 1866, when Governor Musgrave of Newfoundland tried to convince the government to send delegates to London in December, he was ignored.

The governors of New Brunswick and Nova Scotia tried to help make Confederation happen but they did not just tell people what to do. Instead, they tried to convince political leaders that some type of union of the British North American colonies—if not Confederation—was the right thing.

In New Brunswick, Governor Arthur Gordon found that he had no choice but to work with Premier Smith, who had been elected to stop Confederation. Gordon got Smith to accept the idea of a union, even if it was not Confederation. Smith then changed his mind, as some of his party did not want any union at all. Since Smith looked so confused, he had to resign—which led to the election of Tilley and a government that wanted Confederation.

In Nova Scotia, Governor Sir William Fenwick Williams tried to convince William Annand, the leader of the group that didn't want Confederation, to suggest to Tupper that they go to London to meet with delegates from the other colonies and write a new plan for a union. Annand thought about doing this, but the Fenian raid on Indian Island shifted the assembly's support to Tupper and his plans for Confederation.

HOWE MEETS HIS MATCH

People who didn't want Confederation started going to London in 1866. Albert Smith of New Brunswick had arrived in early 1866 to ask the Colonial Office for help. But he was surprised to find that Colonial Secretary Viscount Edward Cardwell was determined to make some sort of union happen. This made him think that union could not be stopped, so he went along with Governor Gordon's sugges-

tion when he got back to New Brunswick in March.

Joseph Howe hoped that he might get more help from the new British government. In June 1866, the Liberal government had lost a vote in the British House of Commons and was forced to dissolve. A Conservative government replaced it, and the Earl of Carnarvon became the new colonial secretary. But nothing changed. Both parties in Britain wanted Confederation to happen. Carnarvon knew that Howe was a powerful political leader in Nova Scotia and did not want him to wreck Confederation. So he told Howe that he would be happy to learn what Howe thought of Confederation and that the British government would not make a final decision until after the 1866 Christmas holidays. At the same time, Macdonald, Cartier, Tupper, Tilley, and the other leaders were busily working on the *British North America (BNA) Act.* Carnarvon wanted

MACDONALD SPENDS CHRISTMAS
IN LONDON, ENGLAND,
WITH HIS NEW WIFE AGNES

to keep Howe busy while the real work was being done.

THE LONDON CONFERENCE

It took several months for all the leaders to arrive in London for the final conference. Tup-per and Tilley left for London on July 19, 1866. Macdonald used the change in the British government as an excuse to stay in North America until November.

Howe was quite busy. In September 1866, he wrote a booklet saying that Confederation was a bad idea. The British did not agree with him.

In October, Howe said that Macdonald was a heavy drinker in an attempt to make Carnarvon think that Confederation was bad because Macdonald was helping to write it. Carnarvon, however, thought that Macdonald was "the best politician in Upper Canada" and ignored Howe.

Howe then thought he had a better idea than Confederation: why not create a worldwide federation in which Great Britain joined with all of its colonies into one big country? Nobody liked this idea. Howe could only wait to see what Macdonald and the others would do.

When the meetings finally began in December, Carnarvon made it clear he wanted the colonists to sort out problems among themselves, which was fine with Macdonald and the others.

Macdonald did most of the writing of the London Conference resolutions, basing them on the Quebec Resolutions. He was very careful to keep everyone happy. He knew that if he changed things too much, Confederation might fall apart.

During this period, Macdonald not only worked on the resolutions, he also met and married his second wife, Agnes. One night, he was working by candlelight in his hotel room, and was so tired that he fell asleep. He woke up to find that the room was on fire. Macdonald was badly burned but continued to work harder than anyone else. On Christmas Day in 1866, Macdonald gave the finished resolutions to the Colonial Office. Joseph Howe wanted to see a copy, but Carnarvon did not give it to him, saying that they were not finished. Howe felt that he had been let down by the British government, which wanted Confederation to happen. Howe would wait to see what form the new country would take.

THE FINAL TOUCHES

In January and February 1867, Macdonald worked with the Colonial Office to write the bill that, when approved by British parliament, would become the *BNA Act*. When bureaucrats in the Colonial Office told him to ignore French Canada and make the provincial governments weak, Macdonald simply ignored them. Macdonald made it clear that this was his bill and that it would be written the way he wanted.

Even so, there were two issues causing concern with the Colonial Office that Macdonald could not just ignore.

First, what was the new country to be called? The delegates to the London Conference all agreed that "Canada" should be the name, even though the

WHAT IF?

CANADA HAD BEEN CALLED BY ANOTHER NAME INSTEAD?

HOW ABOUT **BOREALIA**, WHICH MEANS 'NORTHERN' IN LATIN. WE COULD HAVE BEEN **BOREALIANS!**

THE DELEGATES WANTED TO USE THE NAME **VICTORIALAND**. I THINK THE CITY OF VICTORIA IS QUITE SUFFICIENT.

ANOTHER NAME WAS **MESOPELAGIA**, WHICH MEANS THE 'LAND BETWEEN THE SEAS'.

From sea to shining sea.

IMAGINE SCREAMING " GO TEAM MESOPELAGIA, GO!"

HOW WOULD YOU FEEL IF YOU WOKE UP ONE FINE MORNING AND FOUND YOURSELF INSTEAD OF A CANADIAN, A **TUPONIAN**?–

TUPONIA IS SHORT FOR "THE UNITED PROVINCES OF NORTH AMERICA".

THE BRITISH EDITOR OF THE ECONOMIST (STILL BEING PUBLISHED TODAY) SUGGESTED THAT THE NEW COUNTRY BE CALLED **NORTHLAND**–

The Economist,

IN THE 1950'S, WE DROPPED 'DOMINION'. IT'S JUST 'CANADA' NOW.

IN 1982, WE CHANGED 'DOMINION DAY' TO 'CANADA DAY'. ISN'T THAT BETTER THAN 'HAPPY MESOPELAGIA DAY?

Colonial Office thought that "British North America" would be better.

Queen Victoria wondered if the Maritime delegates really liked the name. Carnarvon was able to assure her that they were the ones who'd suggested it because they thought "it should be known by a name which is at once familiar and important."

This didn't settle the name problem. In the British Empire, a country was given a formal "style" as part of its name. Great Britain's full name was "the United Kingdom of Great Britain and Ireland." What should Canada's formal name be?

Macdonald and the others at first wanted to use the name "the Kingdom of Canada." The British did not like this name, which, they were sure, would upset the United States. So they had to find another style for Canada.

Leonard Tilley is supposed to have suggested that the style be "the Dominion of Canada," based on Psalms 72:8 from the Bible, which refers to "dominion from sea unto sea." This was a good name for a Confederation that hoped to reach the Pacific Ocean. But the name "Dominion" had been used for other British territories before 1867, so Tilley may have only reminded the British

of a name that they felt comfortable with—and that would not upset the United States. No matter—"Dominion of Canada" became the name.

The second issue surprised Macdonald and the other delegates. The British would give Canada complete independence, if the colonists wanted it. The new country did not have to be part of the British Empire at all.

The delegates said no. They had been brought up to think of themselves as British—even French Canadians saw them-

> **THE BRITISH MPs CARED MORE ABOUT HOMELESS DOGS THAN ABOUT THE BRITISH NORTH AMERICA ACT.**

selves as part of the British Empire. They did not want to leave.

They also did not want their new country to become part of the United States. They needed British help to work with the United States, which might not take Canada seriously at first. On its own, Canada was a small, obscure country, but, as part of the British Empire, it was more important.

Besides, if the United States ever did invade Canada, the

new country would need Britain's help to defend itself—and being part of the British Empire might make the Americans think twice.

So Canada would stay in the British Empire.

THE BNA ACT PASSES

In March 1867, the bill was finally ready to be voted on by British parliament. The House of Lords passed the bill on March 12, 1867. On March 27, the British House of Commons passed the bill.

Macdonald was annoyed. Very few members of the House of Commons said anything about the *BNA Act*. But they all argued about the next bill to be voted on—whether to make a shelter for homeless dogs pay tax. D'Arcy McGee made Macdonald feel better by telling him that he would have been furious if they had tried to change his bill.

Queen Victoria signed the bill on March 29. This is called giving the bill "royal assent." At the signing, the Queen made it clear that she was happy with the *BNA Act* and that she thought highly of John A. Macdonald.

The act would come into force on July 1, 1867. That was the day when Canada would be born.

I BRING IN FREE TRADE. I MAKE CANADA RICHER. I TRY TO SAVE THE COUNTRY AFTER TRUDEAU MESSED IT UP. AND THEY STILL CALL ME "LYIN' BRIAN!"

- BRIAN MULRONEY

STATE OF THE UNION?

THE BNA ACT & HOW IT WORKS

The *British North America Act* set out the rules by which Canada works. It is now called the *Constitution Act, 1867*, after the constitution was "patriated," or brought to Canada, in 1982. The rules—and the country—still work very well.

The new country had four provinces: New Brunswick, Nova Scotia, Ontario (the new name for Canada West), and Quebec (the new name for Canada East). Quebec was named for Quebec City. At first, Ontario was going to be named "Toronto" but, even in 1867, enough people disliked the power of Toronto that the new province was called

Federal Government Powers (Section 91)

- raises most of the money from taxes and decides how much money to give to the provinces

- decides what actions would be crimes in Canada;

- runs the penitentiaries for the most dangerous criminals;

- runs the army and navy;

- designs and prints paper money and coins;

- has the power to make laws for the peace, order and good government of Canada, which gives the federal government the power to make laws about anything that has not been listed;

- has the power to disallow or cancel, any provincial law (section 90) within one year of it being passed by a provincial government. This power has not been used since 1943, but it still exists

"Ontario" instead, after Lake Ontario.

The *Constitution Act* set out two levels of government for the Dominion of Canada.

FEDERAL GOVERNMENT

The first level is the federal government. Its powers are listed in Section 91 of the *Constitution Act*. It was meant to be the strongest level of government. The federal government:

- raises most of the money from taxes and decides how much money to give the provinces
- decides what actions would be crimes in Canada
- runs the penitentiaries for the most dangerous criminals

Provincial
Government
Powers
(Section 92 & 93)

– makes the rules that towns and cities must obey. The provinces create cities under section 92 (B);

- runs hospitals;

- runs taverns and bars;

- runs prisons for less dangerous criminals;

- makes the rules under which people can own houses (real property) and things like cars, clothes and mp3 players (personal property);

- makes the rules for students and teachers in schools (section 93)

• The Senate, which is appointed by the prime minister from four regions of Canada: the Maritimes, Ontario, Quebec, and the western provinces. The prime minister also appoints senators from Newfoundland and Labrador, the Northwest Territories, Nunavut, and the Yukon Territory. They are not included in the four regions. Together, the two houses are called the Parliament of Canada.

PROVINCIAL GOVERNMENT

The second level is the provincial government. Its powers are listed in Sections 92–93 of the *Constitution Act*. It was meant to be the weaker level of government. The provincial government:
• makes the rules that towns and cities must obey (provinces create cities and towns)
• runs hospitals, taverns and bars, and prisons
• makes the rules under which people can own houses (real property) and things like cars, clothes, and MP3 players (personal property)
• makes the rules for students and teachers in schools
Provincial governments have only one house: the elected legislative assembly.

The *Constitution Act* also created the Canadian justice system, under Sections 96–101 of the act. The federal government was given the power to create courts, where trials are held, and courts of appeal, including the Supreme Court of Canada, where people who are unhappy with what took

• runs the army and the navy
• has the power to make laws "for the peace, order, and good government of Canada," which gives the federal government the power to make laws about anything that has not been listed
• has the power to disallow, or cancel, any provincial laws within one year of them be-

ing passed by a provincial government.
The federal government is made up of two houses:
• The House of Commons, which is elected by the people. Each province has a certain number of seats in the Commons, based on its population. The more people who live in a province, the more seats it has in the Commons.

THE BNA ACT COMES HOME. 1982

place in a previous trial may argue that the previous court had made a mistake. The provinces can also create courts, but these courts deal with laws about marriage and children, as well as small claims, where one person can ask the court to make another person pay back the money they owe.

The act also included an important part—Section 145—that promised that the Intercolonial Railway would be built. Without this section, New Brunswick and Nova Scotia would not have joined Confederation. The Intercolonial Railway was finished on July 1, 1876.

Most of these rules are still being used today. The main power that has since been

added was given to the federal government. It is the authority to talk to the governments of other countries, such as the United States, about making treaties. This is called "foreign affairs," and Canada got the power in 1931. In 1867, Canadians did not think that they were strong enough yet to talk to the United States without Britain's help, as the United States was so big and Canada was so small.

CHANGING THE CONSTITUTION

Something else was missing. The act didn't say how it could be changed. As time went by, we found that there were other

things—new rules—that we wanted to add to the act.

Because the *British North America Act* was passed by the British parliament, only the British parliament could change it. But Great Britain said it would only change the act if Canadians could agree on the changes that they wanted to make. This was hard to do.

When you are with a lot of your friends, do you always agree about what you are going to do? It's not always easy for everyone to agree.

It was just as bad for the provinces and the federal government. Did every province have to agree to make a change, or only some of them? If every province, as well as the federal government, had to agree, change would be nearly impossible, because it is hard to get all the provinces—and there were 10 by 1949—to agree on anything.

It took a long time for the federal and provincial governments to agree on how to make changes. They tried to create the rules for making changes in 1927, but it took until 1982 for them to succeed. These rules are so tough that it is hard for us to make any changes in how the country works. This is a good thing—

I'M STILL THE ONLY FEMALE PRIME MINISTER – BUT I BET I'LL HAVE COMPANY SOON!

– KIM CAMPBELL

STATE OF THE UNION?

we don't want to wreck the country by mistake.

Still, we should be pleased with how Canada works, even though—like every country—it has problems at times. Canada has one of the oldest governments in the world.

In 1867, many of the countries we think of as older than we are did not exist, or had a different type of government. China and Japan are very old, but their governments today are much younger than Canada's. Japan's government was created in 1947, after World War II, and the current government of China was created in 1949.

In Europe, Germany has had four different types of government since the 1860s: the First Reich (1871–1919), the Weimar Republic (1919–1933), the Third Reich (1933–1945), and the Federal Republic (1949–present). France has

changed its government too. It had the Third Republic (1871–1940), Vichy France under Nazi German control (1940–1945), the Fourth Republic (1945–1958), and the Fifth Republic (1958–present).

> MACDONALD, TUPPER, TILLEY, AND THE OTHERS BUILT BETTER THAN THEY KNEW - OURS IS THE THIRD OLDEST GOVERNMENT IN THE WORLD!

There are only two governments that are older than Canada's. Great Britain's, which began with a king who ruled by himself and gradually became the democracy that our government is based on, is over a thousand years old. The first

British prime minister appeared in 1742. The prime minister and the House of Commons have been stronger than the King or Queen ever since.

The United States government is also older than ours is. It began in 1789, after the states had written and accepted the constitution. It took 13 years, after the Declaration of Independence in 1776, for the Americans to invent a government that would work for them.

Macdonald, Tupper, Tilley, and the others built better than they knew. They wanted to create a new country that would end the political deadlock in the Province of Canada, be able to protect itself from the United States, and allow its people to rule themselves with responsible government. That Canada has lasted so long, and done so well, tells us what a great job they did when they put Canada together.

THEN AND NOW...

THEN, WOMEN COULD ONLY PLAY A ROLE IN POLITICS THROUGH THEIR FATHER OR HUSBAND.

NOW - THINGS HAVE CHANGED!

WOMEN COULD FIRST VOTE IN 1916, IN MANITOBA ELECTIONS. BY 1940, WOMEN COULD VOTE IN ALL FEDERAL AND PROVINCIAL ELECTIONS.

IN 1929, THE PRIVY COUNCIL IN LONDON, ENGLAND DECLARED THAT WOMEN WERE PEOPLE.

NELLIE McCLUNG

Herald
WOMEN ARE PERSONS!

AGNES McPHAIL WAS THE FIRST WOMAN TO BE ELECTED AS A MEMBER OF PARLIAMENT IN OTTAWA.

ELLEN LOUKS FAIRCLOGH WAS THE FIRST WOMAN TO BE NAMED AS A FEDERAL CABINET MINISTER, IN 1957.

IN 1993, KIM CAMPBELL BECAME CANADA'S FIRST FEMALE PRIME MINISTER

24 Sussex Drive

WHO WILL BECOME CANADA'S NEXT FEMALE PRIME MINISTER? MAYBE IT WILL BE A READER OF THIS BOOK.

?

FROM SEA TO SHINING SEA

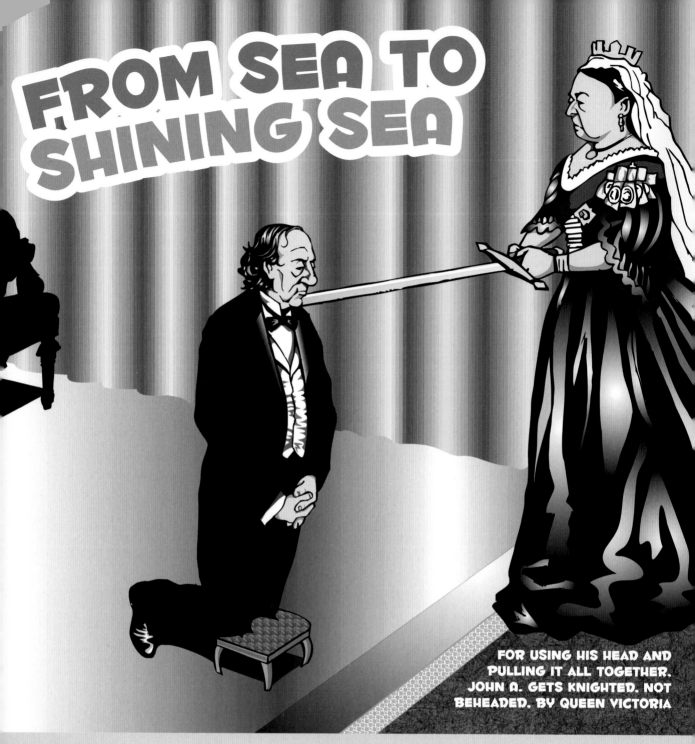

FOR USING HIS HEAD AND PULLING IT ALL TOGETHER, JOHN A. GETS KNIGHTED, NOT BEHEADED, BY QUEEN VICTORIA

John A. Macdonald was pleased with himself on July 1, 1867. The new country was born. He had been chosen to become its first prime minister. Macdonald was sure that his Conservative party would win the first federal elections in September.

Best of all, Macdonald had been honoured by Queen Victoria, who had given him a knighthood. From now on, Macdonald would be called Sir John A. Macdonald. His new wife, Agnes, whom he had met and married just a few months earlier in London, was also delighted. She would be Lady Macdonald. That would make up for life in Ottawa, which was much different from life in the capital of the British Empire.

Macdonald's friends and political allies were not very happy at first. They had not been honoured in the same way. But they all had to admit that Macdonald was the man who had held the conference together, written the *BNA Act*, and worked with the British to get the act passed into law. Macdonald did his best to work with them. One by one, he convinced Tilley, Tupper, Cartier, and others who had helped to create Confederation to come to Ottawa with him to run the new country. Macdonald made sure that they all had important jobs in the new government.

George Brown had left the Great Coalition in 1866 and gone back to running his newspaper, the *Globe*. He thought it was time for the Great Coalition to break up. It had created Confederation and done its job. He wanted to lead his Reform party in the 1867 elections, and win. But he lost to a member of Macdonald's party. Brown would keep running the *Globe*, ready to take on Macdonald in the future.

But problems soon began to appear. Joseph Howe and Nova Scotia were still not happy.

NOVA SCOTIA ACCEPTS CONFEDERATION

In the 1867 elections, Macdonald's Conservative party did well in Ontario, Quebec, and New Brunswick, winning the most seats in each province. But it was different in Nova Scotia, where only one Confederation supporter—Tupper—gained a seat. The other 18 were won by members who wanted Nova Scotia to leave Confederation. Joseph Howe was one of them.

At first, it was not clear that these 18 members would even go to Ottawa to take their seats in the House of Commons, but they all went. They were proud of Nova Scotia, and would represent Nova Scotia, even if they did not like Confederation.

> HOWE JUST WOULD NOT GIVE UP. HE WENT TO LONDON IN 1868 AND ASKED THE BRITISH TO LET NOVA SCOTIA LEAVE CONFEDERATION!

Macdonald was not worried at first. Some historians think that he wanted the Maritimes to join Confederation only to end the political deadlock in the two Canadas, and did not really care what happened in the Maritimes after that. Macdonald was sure he would gain enough seats in Ontario and Quebec that he could win more elections and still be prime minister.

Leonard Tilley had to tell Macdonald that he was wrong, that he could not ignore Howe and Nova Scotia's concerns. Howe was so upset that, in 1868, he went to London and asked the British to let Nova Scotia leave Confederation. The British government said no. Still, how could Canada have any long-term future if people already wanted to leave it?

Macdonald decided to offer Howe and Nova Scotia a deal. He remembered that, unlike New Brunswick, Nova Scotia had not been given any extra federal money when it had agreed to join Confederation. So he offered Howe two things: money for Nova Scotia to spend, and a place for Howe in his cabinet, to help him rule the country.

HOWE AND MACDONALD KISS AND MAKE UP

IF IT WEREN'T FOR ME, CANADA WOULD HAVE BEEN BROKEN UP. YOU HAVE TO SPEN' MONEY TO KEEP CANADA TOGET'ER - JOHN A. KNEW 'DAT!"

- JEAN CHRÉTIEN

STATE OF THE UNION?

GREENLAND
(Denmark)

ALASKA
(Russia)

THE
NORTH WESTERN
TERRITORIES

NEWFOUNDLAND

BRITISH
COLUMBIA

RUPERT'S LAND

PRINCE
EDWARD
ISLAND
NEW   NOVA
BRUNSWICK   SCOTIA

QUEBEC

ONTARIO

UNITED STATES OF AMERICA

IF IT'S GREEN, IT'S CANADA.
IF IT'S NOT, IT'S NOT.

Howe accepted Macdonald's offer, and became a cabinet minister. The extra money, and the place for Howe, helped Nova Scotians to be happy in Confederation. In the 1872 federal election, all the seats in Nova Scotia were won by members who wanted to stay in Canada.

Macdonald had risen to his first big challenge to keep Canada together. He had shown that the new country could work.

CANADA GROWS – BUILDING THE NEW COUNTRY

Other British colonies watched as Canada did well. Some of them wanted to join too.

Canada was very small in 1867. The provinces of Ontario and Quebec were much smaller than they are today. The northern regions were part of Rupert's Land, which was owned by the Hudson's

Bay Company (HBC). In 1670, Great Britain's King Charles II granted this land to the HBC. Rupert's Land also included today's Manitoba, Saskatchewan, southern Alberta, and a portion of the Northwest Territories and Nunavut.

First Nations peoples lived there, but they were not able to stop the many new settlers who were arriving from Canada, Europe, and the United States. Which country was going to control Rupert's Land: Canada or the United States?

George Brown wanted Canada West to expand into Hudson's Bay Company territory, and was sure that one day all of the land in the west would belong to Canada West. Cartier did not like the idea at all. Macdonald, for his part, said that he would be happy to leave the west alone for 50 years, but that if "Englishmen do not go there, Yankees will." Macdonald was right.

The United States government was interested in moving north and west. The Red River Colony was only 80 kilometres from the border of the new state of Minnesota, which had a population of 300,000 people. In 1867, the United States had bought Alaska from Russia for $2,000,000 ($25,000,000 today).

It was already moving soldiers and ships to Alaska.

THE BIRTH OF MANITOBA

The Hudson's Bay Company wanted to sell its land because it could not make money from the fur trade any longer. In 1869, Canada bought the Rupert's Land from the Hudson's Bay Company, and made plans to take over the territory, including the Red River Colony. Canada chose a lieutenant governor, William McDougall, who sent surveyors to study the land. The surveyors ignored the Métis, the people who already lived there.

Louis Riel became leader of the Métis, and did not allow McDougall to come to the colony. Riel created a provisional, or temporary, government. When Canada refused

to take over from the Hudson's Bay Company because of Riel's actions, Riel wanted to talk with the Canadian government about the future of the colony. He wanted the colony to become another province of Canada, to be called Assiniboia.

Macdonald decided that Canada had to negotiate with the provisional government, so Riel sent a team to meet with Macdonald and Cartier in Ottawa.

They were able to reach an agreement. The Manitoba Act, which protected language rights for both the English and French and made sure that there would be schools for both Protestants and Catholics, was passed on May 12, 1870. Manitoba joined Confederation on July 15, 1870. It was called the "postage stamp" province, because it was very small and the shape of a stamp.

LOUIS RIEL HAD NOT EXECUTED THOMAS SCOTT?

RIEL COULD STAY IN MANITOBA AND WELCOME IT'S FIRST LIEUTENANT GOVERNOR, A.G. ARCHIBALD.

RIEL WAS ELECTED TO THE HOUSE OF COMMONS IN 1873, BUT WAS NOW ABLE TO TAKE HIS SEAT AND SERVE AS AN MP.

RIEL HELPS GABRIEL DUMONT AND THE METIS TO SOLVE THEIR LAND DISPUTE WITH OTTAWA. THERE IS NO 1885 REBELLION, AND RIEL IS NOT HANGED FOR LEADING IT.

IN 1886, MACDONALD VISITS RIEL AND DUMONT IN SASKATCHEWAN DURING MACDONALD'S CROSS-CANADA TRIP ON THE NEW CANADIAN PACIFIC RAILWAY

IN 1896, QUEBEC STILL VOTES FOR THE CONSERVATIVE PARTY WHICH IT SEES AS THE PROTECTOR OF FRENCH RIGHTS. WILFRID LAURIER NEVER BECOMES PRIME MINISTER.

THE CONSERVATIVE PARTY IS SEEN AS THE PARTY THAT PROTECTS PEOPLE'S RIGHTS, ESPECIALLY IN QUEBEC. IT WINS ALMOST ALL THE ELECTIONS IN THE 20TH CENTURY.

CANADA SINCE 1999

GREENLAND
(Denmark)

ALASKA
(U. S.)

YUKON
TERRITORY

NORTHWEST
TERRITORIES

NUNAVUT

NEWFOUNDLAND

BRITISH
COLUMBIA

ALBERTA

SASKATCHEWAN

MANITOBA

ONTARIO

QUEBEC

PRINCE
EDWARD
ISLAND

NEW
BRUNSWICK

NOVA
SCOTIA

UNITED STATES OF AMERICA

Unfortunately, Riel was not in Manitoba to celebrate. A number of settlers from Canada, led by Thomas Scott, had fought back against his government. They had been arrested by Riel's government, but continued to cause trouble in jail. Thomas Scott, who disliked the Métis, was put on trial for insulting Riel, refusing to obey the provisional government, and fighting with the men who were guarding him in jail. Scott was found guilty and

was put to death, even though there was no death penalty for these crimes.

After some of Scott's friends broke out of jail and went to Ontario, they told the newspapers what had happened. This made people in Ontario angry. They said that Riel had led a rebellion against Canada, and that he had to be punished for it.

The Canadian government sent soldiers to the new province to show the United States that it

was in control. They arrived on August 24, 1870. Riel had heard that some of the soldiers wanted to beat him up, so he left Manitoba before they arrived.

Still, Riel had helped to create Canada's fifth province. He had protected the rights of the Métis. Other First Nations peoples were not as fortunate. They were not asked about Confederation at all. But the federal government was given the power to deal with First Nations peoples under the *British North America Act*. It would not be until the 20th century that the government of Canada would properly address aboriginal rights.

BRITISH COLUMBIA JOINS CONFEDERATION

The west coast of British North America had not one but two colonies. Vancouver Island had become a British colony in 1849. The British government allowed the Hudson's Bay Company to rent the colony for 10 years, so that it could find ways to increase the number of settlers living there.

In 1857, people thought that there was a lot of gold on the mainland, and 20,000 people came to find it. Britain created the new colony of British Columbia in 1858. More settlers came to British Columbia, and they were soon fighting with the governor, James Douglas, who ruled both Vancouver Island and British Columbia as if he were a king. Many settlers, including leaders such as Amor De Cosmos, wanted the colonies to have responsible government. The settlers, they believed, should rule themselves.

Douglas was retired by Britain in 1864, and Vancouver Island was given responsible government. However, the new governor, Sir Arthur Edward Kennedy, found that the island could not survive on its own, as it could not raise enough money in taxes to pay for the government. In 1866, Vancouver Island joined British Columbia. The two colonies became one.

British Columbia had its own governor, Frederick Seymour, who became the governor of the United Colonies of Vancouver Island and British Columbia. The united colony did not have full responsible government. It had only a legislative council, with eight members chosen by the governor and seven members elected by the people of the colony.

The united colony had problems. The government had to build new roads and schools for the many new settlers, which cost a lot of money. When the gold rush ended, the government could not make enough money from taxes to pay for everything.

British Columbia could not go on as it was, or it would soon be broke. There were really just two choices: join the United States or join the new Confederation.

Many British Columbians felt that joining the United States made a lot of sense now that it had bought Alaska. Joining the United States would bring money and jobs to British Columbia. And

the Americans would be happy to have it join, as it would connect Alaska to the rest of the United States.

But others thought that British Columbia could also remain part of British North America. They were interested in the new Confederation. Amor De Cosmos, a newspaper reporter, and the most prominent newspaper, the *British Colonist*, printed news about what was happening in the east. The *Colonist* thought Confederation was a great idea, and from 1864 to 1867 printed many articles to make sure that the colonists knew that a new country was being born in the east. Amor De Cosmos even set up the Confederation League to urge the people of British Columbia to join Confederation.

Neither British Columbia nor Vancouver Island had delegates at the conferences in 1864. They could not afford to send them, and they were not sure that Macdonald and the others—except for Brown—were even interested in having the two colonies join Confederation. It was only after news of the conferences reached the west

CANADA, THE SHAPE-SHIFTER

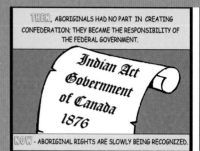

THEN, ABORIGINALS HAD NO PART IN CREATING CONFEDERATION; THEY BECAME THE RESPONSIBILITY OF THE FEDERAL GOVERNMENT.

Indian Act
Government
of Canada
1876

NOW - ABORIGINAL RIGHTS ARE SLOWLY BEING RECOGNIZED.

UNDER THE INDIAN ACTS, NATIVES WERE MOVED TO TRY TO IMPROVE THEIR LIVING CONDITIONS OR BECAUSE THERE WERE RESOURCES ON THEIR LANDS THAT NON NATIVES WANTED TO USE.

JOHN DIEFENBAKER BELIEVED IN ABORIGINAL RIGHTS SINCE HIS BOYHOOD. HE FOUGHT TO GIVE THEM THE RIGHT TO VOTE.

Proclamation
Aboriginals given the right to vote
March 10, 1960

THE 1974 BERGER COMMISSION WAS THE FIRST CHANCE THAT ABORIGINALS HAD TO TELL CANADIANS ABOUT HOW BADLY THEY HAD BEEN TREATED.

BERGER COMMISION

IN 1982, AFTER MANY YEARS OF STRUGGLE, ABORIGINAL RIGHTS WERE RECOGNIZED AND GUARANTEED UNDER OUR CONSTITUTION.

Charter of Rights
section 25

The Charter shall not abrogate or derogate any aboriginal rights or freedoms.

IN 1997, THE SUPREME COURT WROTE THE RULES ABOUT ABORIGINAL OWNERSHIP OF LAND. THE COURT WANTS ABORIGINALS AND GOVERNMENTS TO MEET TO SETTLE THEIR DISAGREEMENTS OVER LAND.

Delgamuukw

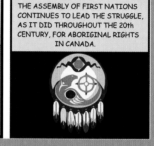

THE ASSEMBLY OF FIRST NATIONS CONTINUES TO LEAD THE STRUGGLE, AS IT DID THROUGHOUT THE 20TH CENTURY, FOR ABORIGINAL RIGHTS IN CANADA.

coast that some people began to get interested in the idea.

By 1867, things had become so bad that the legislative council passed a motion, which all the members voted for, that British Columbia join Canada.

It would not be easy. How would the two be connected? It was much easier to travel to the eastern United States, as there was already a railway joining the east coast of the United States with its west coast. A railway would have to be built connecting Ontario with British Columbia, or there would be no reason for it to join Confederation.

Still, if the people of British Columbia wanted to stay British and not join the United States, they would have to join Canada.

British Columbia finally got responsible government in 1866, which helped De Cosmos in his fight to join Canada.

He was elected to the first legislative assembly from 1867 to 1868 and again from 1870 to 1871. He worked with the newly appointed Governor Musgrave, and with Leonard Tilley, the minister of customs in the Canadian government, to bring British Columbia into Confederation.

It took two years, but British Columbia became part of Canada on July 25, 1871. Canada would pay off the money that its new province owed, and promised to build a railway to connect it with Ontario. The railway took another 14 years to finish, but finally opened for travel on June 28, 1886.

PEI JOINS CONFEDERATION

Prince Edward Island had decided not to join Confedera-

tion in 1867. In the early 1870s, its government had decided to build a railway from one end of the island to the other. The railway cost a lot of money, though, and PEI did not have enough to pay for it. By 1873, things were so bad that the island had to ask the British Colonial Office for help. When the Colonial Office turned it down, PEI's government looked to the United States. Macdonald did not want the Americans to have anything to do with Prince Edward Island, so he worked out a deal: the Canadian government would pay for the railway, buy land from the remaining absentee landlords—many of whom had sold their land to the farmers by 1873—and set up year-round contact with mainland Canada. Prince Edward Island joined Confederation on July 1, 1873.

THE 20TH CENTURY – NEW PROVINCES AND TERRITORIES

After Canada took possession of Rupert's Land in 1870, the area between Manitoba and the Rocky Mountains was called the Northwest Territories. The population rose in great leaps as immigrants from Europe and the United States continued to pour onto the Prairies and into its towns. Local political leaders wanted more powers from Ottawa to serve the population better. As a result, in 1905, the provinces of Alberta and Saskatchewan were formed out of four districts of the Northwest Territories.

In 1949, Newfoundland and Labrador joined Confederation at long last. Newfoundland had become a dominion—like Canada—in 1907, but the Great Depression of the 1930s affected it so badly that it became a British colony again in 1934. World War II revived the Newfoundland economy, and Newfoundlanders had to decide if they wanted to become a dominion again, remain a colony, or join Confederation. They held two referendums to decide. In the first, on June 3, 1948, they concluded that they did not want to be a colony anymore, but could not decide between joining Confederation or becoming a dominion.

In the second, held July 22, 1948, Newfoundlanders decided by a vote of 52–48 per cent to join Canada. Newfoundland became Canada's 10th province on March 31, 1949.

There were changes in the Northwest Territories as well. The Yukon Territory was created in 1898, because of the Klondike gold rush. In 1978, the Yukon was given responsible government. In 2003, its government was given powers that made it nearly as powerful as a provincial government.

Nunavut became Canada's newest territory on April 1, 1999. It is not a province, though it has its own premier and legislative assembly. The remaining Northwest Territories also have their own premier and legislative assembly. A commissioner is chosen by the federal government to represent it, much as the governor general represents the Queen in Canada. Commissioners have very little power and do not interfere with the territorial governments.

The three territories get their powers from the federal government, while the provinces get their powers from the *British North America Act*. Many people in the territories think that they should become provinces, but we would have to change the constitution to do this. Some of the 10 provinces we have now do not want the territories to join them, so this will not happen in the near future.

FROM SEA UNTO SEA – UNTO SEA

By 1871, Canada had become a nation stretching from the Atlantic to the Pacific to the Arctic. It was the second biggest country on earth. And the federal government was set to become the strongest government in Canada.

But Macdonald found that some of the provinces didn't like being so weak. Ontario did not think that it had to bow down to the federal government and do whatever it wanted it to do. One person—the man Macdonald thought he had gotten rid of, Oliver Mowat—had come back to politics, and was ready to fight Macdonald for power.

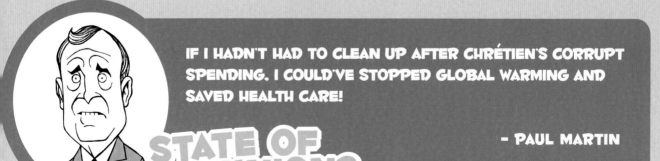

IF I HADN'T HAD TO CLEAN UP AFTER CHRÉTIEN'S CORRUPT SPENDING, I COULD'VE STOPPED GLOBAL WARMING AND SAVED HEALTH CARE!

– PAUL MARTIN

STATE OF THE UNION?

WHO'S STRONGER?

From the start, John A. Macdonald wanted the federal government to be much stronger than the provinces. He made sure the *BNA Act* included the power to disallow provincial laws.

Macdonald disallowed 46 laws. The provinces did not like this, but Macdonald said that the power was in the constitution and he was going to use it.

Oliver Mowat, who had helped to write the resolutions at Quebec that included the disallowance power, thought Macdonald was misusing it. Unfortunately for Macdonald, Mowat was no longer a judge—he was now the premier of Ontario and could fight back.

The fight really began over Ontario's northwestern boundary. When Manitoba was created in 1870, it was small. The Northwest Territories were large and both Ontario and Manitoba wanted some of this land.

Prime Minister Alexander Mackenzie had chosen an arbitration panel to make the decision. The land had been given to the

MOWAT: "BRING IT ON, MACDONALD!"

Hudson's Bay Company in 1670, based on certain rules. Mowat was able to show that, under those rules, the land should go to Ontario. The panel members agreed. But before Mackenzie could make a law giving the land to Ontario, he lost the prime minister's seat to Macdonald in the 1878 election.

Macdonald wanted to give all the land north and west of Port Arthur and Fort William—today's Thunder Bay—to Manitoba.

Macdonald thought that Ontario was already too strong and did not want to give it more land and resources. Macdonald wanted the land and resources for the federal government. In the *Manitoba Act*, it had been made clear that the federal government would own all the minerals—gold and oil—in Manitoba. Ontario, on the other hand, owned all minerals in its territory.

Mowat ignored Macdonald. His government made a law that gave the land to Ontario, and sent surveyors and inspectors. Macdonald was furious. On March 21, 1881, his government made a different law that gave all the land to Manitoba.

Mowat was angry now too. On January 26, 1882, he said that Ontario would leave Confederation if it were not fairly treated. The argument over the land went on. In 1883, Mowat won the Ontario election, saying that if he won, he would make sure Ontario got the land. Mowat sent police to the territory. Macdonald sent police as well. They spent time arresting each other as a "danger to the peace."

Manitoba decided that it wanted Ontario to have the land. It was not good farmland and, in any event, the province would not own the minerals underneath it. Manitoba and Ontario decided to take the dispute to court,

as Macdonald and Mowat could not settle it themselves. One of the court's jobs is to tell the governments of Canada how the constitution works.

Macdonald thought that the federal government was stronger than the provinces, and said so. Didn't it have the power to disallow provincial laws? And, by the way, hadn't Mowat agreed to that at the Quebec Conference?

> BOTH MACDONALD AND MOWAT SENT POLICE TO THE TERRITORY. THE RESULT: THE POLICE ARRESTED EACH OTHER!

Mowat said that he hadn't. The only reason he'd let Macdonald put disallowance into the Quebec Resolutions, Mowat said, was because it could not be used—at all.

Mowat argued that, under responsible government, an elected government had the right to make laws. The *BNA Act* gave the provinces the power to make laws about things listed in Section 92. How, then, could the federal government overrule laws made by a responsible government using its powers under the constitution?

Mowat said that the provinces—as Upper Canada/Canada West, Lower Canada/Canada East, Nova Scotia, and New Brunswick—had existed before Confederation. The federal government hadn't begun until 1867.

The provinces had given the federal government the powers that were listed in Section 91, and no others. Mowat thought that the provinces were equal to the federal government. He was one of the best lawyers in Canada, and presented his side to the judges himself.

Mowat won. The judges thought he was right. Confederation was made up of provinces that had given only certain powers to the federal government. The provinces could make the laws they wanted under the list of powers in Section 92 and the federal government could not cancel them.

Canada was changed forever. The provinces would not get weaker and fade away, as Macdonald had hoped. Instead, they were as strong as, and equal to, the federal government. In the 20th and 21st centuries, when the people of Canada wanted more and better education and health care, the provinces seemed to be more important than the federal government for the future of Canada.

Macdonald would have been upset by the growth of the provinces. But it was his own fault. Macdonald was not as smart—or as good a lawyer—as Oliver Mowat.

Perhaps Mowat's idea was better. The provinces have been able to protect their people because they are so strong. Might a dominant federal government have driven Ontario and Quebec to leave Canada long ago?

THE WEST WILL PLAY A BIG PART IN CANADA'S FUTURE.

- STEPHEN HARPER

STATE OF THE UNION?

MAPLE LEAF FOREVER

Sir Adams George Archibald

George Brown

Sir Alexander Campbell

Sir Frederick Carter

Sir George-Étienne Cartier

Edward Chandler

Jean-Charles Chapais

James Cockburn

George Coles

Robert B. Dickey

Charles Fisher

Sir Alexander Galt

John Hamilton Gray

Thomas Haviland

William Henry

William Howland

John Mercer Johnson

John Hamilton Gray

Sir Hector-Louis Langevin

Andrew Macdonald

Sir John A. Macdonald

Jonathan McCully

William McDougall

Thomas D'Arcy McGee

Peter Mitchell

Sir Oliver Mowat

Edward Palmer

William Henry Pope

John William Ritchie

Sir Ambrose Shea

William H. Steeves

Sir Étienne-Paschal Taché

Sir Samuel Tilley

Sir Charles Tupper

Edward Whelan

Robert Duncan Wilmot

THE CANADA 36: FATHERS OF CONFEDERATION

Many people dreamt about what Canada could be. Macdonald, Brown, Cartier, Tupper, Tilley, De Cosmos, Mowat, and many others worked to create and build Confederation. It is no surprise that the Canada they created does not look exactly the way Macdonald wanted it to be, or Mowat, or Howe, or Tilley, or Tupper. Canada was built by people who knew that all contributions were important if the country was to last. The creators of Confederation had to ensure that everyone could benefit in some way from joining the new country.

Perhaps that founding lesson is why Canada has survived and grown while other countries have had to change their governments many times over the years. We learned from the beginning that a country must respect the rights of others if it's to last for a long time.

We learned, as well, that there are ways to settle arguments without fighting. People can talk and reach agreement. If they have to, they can go to the courts, whose job it is to settle arguments. In many other countries, rulers can and will ignore court decisions they don't like. But Macdonald, who hated losing to Mowat, knew he had to obey the court's decision. He accepted that Canada was not going to have the strong federal government he wanted. Canada became a very different country from the one that Macdonald thought it should be.

Yet, Canada did become the country Macdonald had hoped to build. The people rule themselves by electing governments, which they can kick out if they don't like. The people have rights that are protected by law. Minority rights are recognized and protected. Most importantly, Canada is still here. The great dream of a country stretching from sea to sea, independent from the United States, has not only survived—it has grown strong and proud.

That dream—that people are smart enough to rule themselves while respecting the rights of others, even if they disagree with them—is special. It makes Canada a great country.

But Canada is still not finished. It never will be. There will always be new challenges and new dreams … and new people to welcome to the Canadian dream.

GLOSSARY

Bleus: led by George-Étienne Cartier, political party formed in 1850 in Canada East. Members believed that they should co-operate with British colonists to ensure that their language and culture survived. They believed that confederating with English-speaking colonies would result in the old Province of Quebec being re-established. The name bleu was chosen to distinguish the party from the Parti rouge. The party allied itself with the Conservative Party in Canada West and together they formed the basis for the future Conservative Party of Canada.

British North America: the name given to all of Great Britain's colonies in North America (the Province of Canada, New Brunswick, Nova Scotia, Newfoundland, Prince Edward Island, British Columbia and the Northwest Territories).

British Empire: lands around the world colonized by Great Britain.

British North America Act, 1867: the Act of the British Parliament that created Canada.

Canada East: the name given to Quebec from 1841 to 1867.

Canada West: the name given to Ontario from 1841 to 1867.

Civil War: the war between the northern and southern states from 1861 to 1865.

Confederacy: the southern states during the Civil War in the United States.

Confederation: the name given to the creation of Canada.

Conservatives: political party in Canada West led by John A. Macdonald. It worked with the Bleus in Canada East.

Constitution: the highest set of laws in Canada. It is a mixture of laws that are written down and laws that are not written down, or traditions. It describes Canada's system of government and the rights of all Canadian citizens.

division of powers: the federal government can make some rules while the provincial governments can make others.

disallowance: the ability of the federal government to stop a provincial government from making a law or rule.

Dominion: the name given to a self-governing colony in the British Empire, such as Canada.

Fenians: a group of Irish-Americans who wanted to free Ireland from British rule.

Fenian Raids: attacks on New Brunswick and the Province of Canada by Fenians in 1866 to try to force Britain to free Ireland.

First Nations: the descendants of the first inhabitants of North America. The Canadian Constitution recognizes three groups of aboriginal (or, earliest known) people: Indians, Métis and Inuit. These are three separate groups of people with unique heritages, languages, cultural practises and spiritual beliefs.

governor: each colony had a governor, who was chosen by the British to represent Britain. Before the 1840s, the governor ruled the colony.

Grand Trunk Railway: a railway network based in the Province of Canada.

Great Coalition: formed by George Brown, George-Étienne Cartier, and John A. Macdonald to break the deadlock in the Province of Canada's Legislative Assembly and create Confederation.

House of Commons: since 1867, the lower house of Parliament. It consists of a Speaker, the prime minister and his Cabinet, members of the governing party, members of the opposition parties, and sometimes a few Independents (elected members who do not belong to an official party). The members of the House (Members of Parliament or MPs) are elected by the Canadian people.

Hudson's Bay Company: the business incorporated in England in 1670 to conduct fur trade with the First Nations people and control all lands whose rivers and streams drained into Hudson Bay. This huge area, called Rupert's Land, stretched from Labrador, across modern day Quebec and Ontario, to south of the present US/Canada border and west to the Canadian Rocky Mountains. In 1870, the company transferred most of its land to the Canadian government.

Intercolonial Railway: the railway which connected New Brunswick and Nova Scotia to Montreal and Toronto.

Judicial Committee of the Privy Council: in London, England. Before 1949 it was the last court of appeal in Canada.

Legislative Assembly: the group of elected representatives that governed the colonies prior to Confederation.

Legislative Council: a group of elected members of the Legislative Assembly chosen by the governor to advise him. This council approved bills passed by the Assembly and could introduce bills itself.

Lower Canada: the southern area of present-day Quebec from 1791 to 1841.

Loyalists: people who came to British North America from the USA after the American Revolution so that they could still live in British territory.

Maritime Union: a proposal to join the Maritimes into one large colony.

Maritimes: the group of colonies that included New Brunswick, Nova Scotia, Prince Edward Island and Newfoundland as a group.

Métis: the people whose ancestry is half First Nations and half European, but mainly French Canadian.

ministry: the name given to the government formed by a party or parties in the Legislative Assembly.

Northwest Rebellion: this was led by Louis Riel in 1885 to protect the rights of natives in what is now Saskatchewan.

Province of Canada: the name given to the combined colonies of Canada East and Canada West from 1841 to 1867.

provincial government: the government of a province, such as Ontario or Alberta.

premier: the leader of a provincial government.

prime minister: the leader of the government of Canada.

Reciprocity Treaty: an 1854–1866 trade agreement between the Province of Canada and the USA.

Reform Party: political party in Canada West that led the opposition to the ruling Conservatives and campaigned for responsible government (more control for the elected members of the government). Led by George Brown, the party formed a short-lived government in the Province of Canada with the Parti rouge of Canada East in 1858. Following Confederation in 1867, the Reform Party merged with the Parti rouge to form the Liberal Party.

Red River Colony: the colony that became Manitoba in 1870.

responsible government: members of the Legislative Assembly, elected by the people, make the rules and govern instead of the governor who was chosen by Britain.

representation by population (Rep by Pop): the number of members that each colony had in the Legislative Assembly was based on the size of the colony's population; the bigger the population, the more elected representatives would sit in the Legislative Assembly.

Rouges: party in Canada East led by Antoine–Aimé Dorion. It was formed in 1848 in Canada East by young intellectual francophones. Members of the party, called les rouges, wanted to undo the Act of the Union, 1841, which united Upper and Lower Canada into a single colony, the Province of Canada. Also, les rouges wanted to have Canada East annexed to the USA. After Confederation, the Parti rouge merged with the Reform Party from Canada West to form the Liberal Party.

Senate: since 1867, it is the upper house of Parliament. Here, senators examine and revise legislation from the House of Commons, investigate national issues and represent regional, provincial and minority interests. The Senate can also introduce its own bills.

Supreme Court of Canada: since 1947, the highest court for all issues in Canada.

Tenant League: a group of farmers who wanted to protect the rights of Prince Edward Island's farmers from the owners of their farms, who lived in Britain.

Upper Canada: the southern area of present-day Ontario from 1791 to 1841.

POLITICAL LEADERS

George Brown (1818–1880): the leader of the Reformers in Canada West, he joined the Great Coalition in 1864 and led the fight for Confederation.

Sir George-Étienne Cartier (1814–1873): the leader of the Bleus in Canada East, he joined the Great Coalition in 1864 and led the fight for Confederation.

George Coles (1810–1875): the premier of Prince Edward Island three times in the 1850s and 1860s, he supported Confederation at first but changed his mind when he saw Confederation would not help his colony.

Amor De Cosmos (1825–1897): born William Alexander Smith, he was a journalist and politician who led the fight for responsible government in British Columbia and led the movement to have the colony join Confederation.

Antoine-Aimé Dorion (1818–1891): the leader of the Rouges in Canada East, he did not like the Confederation idea and did not join the Great Coalition.

Joseph Howe (1804–1873): premier of Nova Scotia from 1860 to 1863. He did not want to join Confederation and only reluctantly accepted it in 1868.

Abraham Lincoln (1809–1865): sixteenth president of the United States of America. He led the North to victory in the Civil War, and freed the slaves in the Emancipation Proclamation of 1863.

Alexander Mackenzie (1822–1892): the second prime minister of Canada (1873–1878).

Sir John A. Macdonald (1815–1891): leader of the Conservatives in Canada West, he joined the Great Coalition in 1864 and led the fight for Confederation. He became the first prime minister of Canada in 1867.

Thomas D'Arcy McGee (1825–1868): author and politician, he is the only Canadian political figure to be assassinated.

Sir Oliver Mowat (1820–1903): premier of Ontario from 1872 to 1896. Mowat fought Macdonald over the power of the federal government to tell the provinces what to do.

Louis Riel (1844–1885): Métis leader and founder of Manitoba. He led the Red River Rebellion in 1869 and the Northwest Rebellion in 1885.

Sir Albert Smith (1822–1868): political leader of New Brunswick who did not want to join Confederation.

Sir Samuel Leonard Tilley (1818–1879): leader of the New Brunswick Reformers, he led the fight for Confederation in New Brunswick.

Sir Charles Tupper (1821–1915): leader of the Nova Scotia Conservatives, he led the fight for Confederation in Nova Scotia.

Queen Victoria (1819–1901): the monarch who signed the British North America Act in 1867.

Edward Whelan (1824–1867): a strong supporter of Confederation in Prince Edward Island who thought that Confederation would give his colony more control over the absentee landlords who controlled its land.

INDEX

STILL WANT TO KNOW MORE? ??

IF YOU WOULD LIKE TO LEARN MORE ABOUT THE PEOPLE AND EVENTS THAT SHAPED CONFEDERATION, YOU MIGHT BE INTERESTED IN:

THESE BOOKS:

Sir John A. Macdonald: The Rascal Who Built Canada
by Jacqueline A. Brown (Toronto: JackFruit Press, 2006)

Reminiscences of Canada
by Mercy Ann Coles. Prince Edward Island Public Archives, 1864.

Sir Oliver Mowat
by A. Margaret Evans (Toronto: University of Toronto Press, 1992)

Sir Charles Tupper: The Bully Who Battled For Canada
by Johanna Bertin (Toronto: JackFruit Press, 2007)

THESE WEBSITES:

LIBRARY AND ARCHIVES CANADA'S TWO WEBSITES:

[a] For all ages:
http://www.collectionscanada.ca/confederation/index-e.html

[b] Confederation for Kids:
http://www.collectionscanada.ca/confederation/kids/index-e.html

THE CANADIAN ENCYCLOPEDIA
[including the Junior Encyclopedia of Canada]

http://www.thecanadianencyclopedia.com/

ABOUT THE AUTHOR!!

PAUL KEERY, B.A., B.ED., LL.B., M.L.I.S.

Paul has an extensive teaching background in Canadian history and politics. His training in Canadian law includes an understanding of constitutional law and the struggles faced by Canadian leaders who must contend with constitutional disputes. A fun and futuristic teacher for 19 years and counting, Paul has also received the international honour of being selected to be an Apple Distinguished Educator, class of 2007.

ABOUT THE ILLUSTRATOR!!

MIKE WYATT

Mike is a self-taught illustrator and a graphic artist. His cartoons and comics have appeared in newspapers thoughout western Canada and his original designs can be seen on everything from hockey jerseys to greeting cards. As an avid history buff, the chance to depict the greats and not so greats of a by-gone era, Warts & All, has been a thoroughly enjoyable experience. He lives in Maple Ridge, BC with his wife Janet, son Tyler and daughter Madeline.